ADVANCE PRAISE FOR

Thank You, Sisters

I heartily recommend *Thank You, Sisters*, and hasten to include my own personal gratitude and praise to the Sisters of Notre Dame de Namur, who taught with great humor and compassion and helped form my conscience at Holy Trinity Parish and School in Dayton, Ohio. Thank you, Sisters, indeed.

—Martin Sheen, actor

There are books which are written and there are books which need to be written. This is one of the latter. And yet it did not really need to be written, because anyone with eyes already knows it is true. This book is just pure celebration and gratitude!

—Richard Rohr, O.F.M.,

author, *Breathing Under Water: Spirituality and the Twelve Steps*

Thank you, Sisters is an exciting tribute to the Sisters of the various religious communities in America. It is important that the whole Church and others are made aware of just what our Sisters have been doing for the past three hundred years, not just here in the United States but also as they have gone out from home into dangerous areas of the world to faithfully carry Jesus's message to the poor and work for justice for the downtrodden. This is a glorious tribute to these brave women.

—Rev. Joseph Girzone,

author, *Joshua: A Parable for Today*

Thank You, Sisters

Stories of
Women Religious
and
How They Enrich
Our Lives

EDITED BY
JOHN FEISTER

Franciscan
MEDIA
Cincinnati, Ohio

Excerpts from, "Saints in the Family," copyright 2012 Steven and Cokie Roberts, distributed by Universal Uclick for UFS, adapted and reprinted by permission. Excerpts from Maureen Orth's essay, "Sister Janet," reprinted with permission of the author. Some segments of Liz Scott Monaghan's essay, "Look Out for Nuns," were originally published in *New Orleans Magazine.* They are used here with permission of the publisher. Scripture passages have been taken from *New Revised Standard Version Bible,* copyright ©1989 by the Division of Christian Education of the National Council of the Churches of Christ in the U.S.A., and used by permission.

Cover design by Kathleen Lynch | Black Kat Design
Photo © Yuji Sakai | Getty Images
Book design by Mark Sullivan

LIBRARY OF CONGRESS CATALOGING-IN-PUBLICATION DATA
Feister, John.
Thank you, sisters : stories of women religious and how they enrich our lives / John Feister.
p. cm.
Includes bibliographical references and index.
ISBN 978-1-61636-532-5 (alk. paper)
1. Monastic and religious life of women—United States—Anecdotes. 2. Leadership Conference of Women Religious of the United States. I. Title.
BX4210.F45 2013
271'.90073—dc23
                    2012038615

ISBN 978-1-61636-532-5
Copyright ©2013, John Feister. All rights reserved.

Published by Franciscan Media
28 W. Liberty St.
Cincinnati, OH 45202
www.FranciscanMedia.org

Printed in the United States of America.
Printed on acid-free paper.
13 14 15 16 17   5 4 3 2 1

To Sisters everywhere,
who inspire us again and again

In April, 2012, the central administration of the Catholic Church announced the results of a three-year "doctrinal assessment" of the fifty-five-year-old organization composed of women who lead 80 percent of the 59,000 Catholic Sisters in the United States. A result of that assessment was the appointment of three U.S. bishops to take over the administration of this organization, the Leadership Conference of Women Religious (LCWR), for five years in order to reform the organization. It was a big surprise to many.

An uproar followed, with Catholics taking sides for and against the Sisters and the Vatican's Congregation for the Doctrine of the Faith (the CDF, which oversaw the assessment and is overseeing implementation of its recommendations). The general public, kept abreast of the story by national media, perhaps mostly thought, "Here we go again—those Catholic bishops, this time picking on the nuns." It was not a pretty time for many Catholics, who felt betrayed seeing their male Church leadership going after their trusted Catholic Sisters.

When I first heard about the assessment results, I was really surprised. I sat down with my wife a few times over the next several days and made a list of thirty-five Catholic Sisters who have truly been formative in our lives. And I knew of many others who could share their own, though likely shorter, lists.

It occurred to us that most people—though by no means all—who have had such positive experiences with Sisters are probably older than, say, forty-five. The 1960s and 1970s marked a major change in church and culture that opened opportunities for women in new places. The convent was no longer the only game in town for Catholic women to find a place to serve outside traditional family life. There was a mass exodus of Sisters away from religious communities and a major decline in recruiting new ones as women began to flourish, not only in homes, but also elsewhere in society.

Younger Catholics today have far less chance of having ever met, been educated by, or worked with a Catholic Sister than did their parents. Sisters simply are more likely to work and live in the background today. The nostalgic caricatures found in movies such as *Blues Brothers* and *Sister Act*, still out there on Netflix, are just that. Huge numbers of the real Sisters who stayed on in spite of the exodus finally have retired and are living prayerful lives in convents, motherhouses, and retirement homes. Many others work outside the public eye, in situations among society's various outcasts.

So, I thought, why not tell some positive stories of the profound influence these women have had on people's lives? Rather than have the Sisters tell their own stories—they're not prone to bragging—I chose to depend on people whose lives they've influenced.

From the famous to the everyday, people around the country could tell of the way these remarkable women have changed their lives and communities. I chose some writers you may recognize, others who've worked with Sisters you may have heard of, and others who just have good Sister stories to tell. I introduce the author at the end of each essay; there is more complete biographical information at the book's end.

May this book inspire other tellings, so that the contribution of Sisters be more widely known. As Father Jim Martin, SJ, said so effectively, when his April 2012 Twitter comments fueled an outpouring of goodwill that, indeed, led to this book, "Thank you, Sisters."

—John Feister, Feast of the Guardian Angels, October 2, 2012

I would like to acknowledge a few people instrumental in making this book. The first inspiration came from my wife, Cathy, whose blood sister, Mary Bookser, SC, has been a lifelong support and inspiration first to Cathy, then to both of us. Cathy and I came up with a list of Sister-friends together, with blogging in mind. My coworkers at Franciscan Media saw a book in the list and saw expanding the list beyond my experience into the form of this book. My dear friend and colleague Judy Ball encouraged and helped refine the idea. James Martin, SJ, whose positive, uplifting, and quick response to support the Sisters when they came under question showed the way for many of us, urged me on when I told him of the idea. Thank you to the contributors, most of whom worked on very short deadlines. Finally, I thank the Franciscan friars, whose widely published statement of support for the Sisters, in June 2012, empowered many of us to move forward.

These are the abbreviations for religious orders found in this book:

CND	Sisters of the Congregation of Notre Dame
C.Ss.R.	Congregation of the Most Holy Redeemer (men), commonly known as Redemptorists
DC	Daughters of Charity
FSPA	Franciscan Sisters of Perpetual Adoration
IHM	Sisters, Servants of the Immaculate Heart of Mary
OFM	Order of Friars Minor (men), commonly known as Franciscans
OP	Order of Preachers, commonly known as Dominicans
RSM	Religious Sisters of Mercy
SC	Sisters of Charity
SNDdeN	Sisters of Notre Dame de Namur
SJ	Society of Jesus (men), commonly known as Jesuits
SSJ	Sisters of St. Joseph

Other Sisters' orders appear in the essays without abbreviation.

Saints in the Family

COKIE ROBERTS AND STEVEN V. ROBERTS

In August of 2012, Sister Pat Farrell, then-president of the Leadership Conference of Women Religious, told a National Public Radio interviewer that there's a reason Sisters don't see the world in black and white: "Women religious stand in very close proximity to people at the margins, to people with very painful, difficult situations in their lives. That is our gift to the Church."

It's a gift women religious have been giving the Church and the country since they landed on this soil almost three hundred years ago. But it's a gift the men in charge—both ecclesiastical and civil—have repeatedly rejected. What the nuns face today is nothing new. Their centuries-long determination to give voice to the powerless—those at the margins—has often met obstinate opposition.

In 1727, the Ursulines were sent to New Orleans to set up hospitals for French soldiers stationed there. But within a year they had established a school where they not only taught the children of elite French planters, but also instructed blacks and Native Americans. Soon they opened an orphanage as well.

Thousands of miles from their bishop, the Ursulines could work without much interference. Rose Philippine Duchesne, who brought the Society of the Sacred Heart to America, was not that lucky. Though promised by the bishop that she would be working with the Indians, after her harrowing voyage in 1818, Mother Duchesne learned the prelate had other plans. He dispatched her to St. Charles, Missouri, telling her it was the city of the future, that St. Louis would never amount to anything.

Despite the difficulty in attracting students to the one-horse town, within weeks Mother Duchesne opened the first free school west of the Mississippi River, paid for by income from the boarding school for wealthy girls. When the bishop refused to allow her to include girls of color, Philippine taught them privately, sending letters home decrying racism.

Elizabeth Ann Seton, who started the first indigenous religious order in the United States, in 1809, and is credited with creating the parochial school system, wrote repeatedly to her bishop about obstacles put in her path by priests overseeing her fledgling community. Though her "want of confidence in [her] Superiors" impeded her work, Mother Seton still managed to open orphanages, hospitals, and schools to serve people on the margins.

Later in the century Katharine Drexel founded a religious order with the mission of ministering to blacks and Native Americans, and she used her considerable personal inheritance to fund it. Meeting with vigorous, sometimes violent opposition, both from priests and politicians, she established schools and churches for African Americans and supported legal challenges to Jim Crow laws.

Frances Cabrini came to this country in 1889 to work with desperately poor Italian immigrants. Even though the archbishop of New York would not allow her to raise money from the Irish or other better-off Catholics, he objected to a wealthy Italian benefactress's plans for an orphanage, huffing that "she is not a bishop and doesn't feel the weight of business responsibility." He thought Mother Cabrini should return to Italy.

Instead she stayed and became the first American citizen to be canonized by the Catholic Church. In fact, the refusal of all of these women to abandon those on the margins—Duchesne, Drexel, Seton,

Cabrini—earned each of them sainthood. The men they did battle with? Not even close.

The bishops would do well to study these lives of the saints. It's a litany that informs and inspires women religious today, who daily strive to follow the tough nuns who came before them. And though the Sisters face difficult choices, they have saints in the family to guide them.

....

Cokie Roberts has won countless awards in broadcast journalism over forty years, including three Emmys, and citation as one of the fifty greatest women in the history of broadcasting. Though most know her from National Public Radio and ABC News, she and her husband, Steven V. Roberts, write a weekly newspaper column syndicated by United Media. This essay, which Cokie offered for this book, is adapted from one of those columns. Cokie's mother, Lindy Boggs, was U.S. Ambassador to the Vatican from 1997 to 2001.

Look Out for Nuns: Sister Helen Prejean

LIZ SCOTT MONAGHAN

It was important to remember, in the summer of 1955, to sit on the right-hand side of the bus. We had to be on the lookout for nuns.

Mary Salisbury and I were twelve years old. We took the bus to the public swimming pool in uptown New Orleans almost every day. And we wore shorts over our bathing suits. Short shorts. Even though the nuns told us, very clearly, that short shorts were an occasion of sin.

Now, we weren't bad girls. We wore scapular medals pinned inside our bathing suits, so that should count for something. But it was hot, and we liked boys, and short shorts were the thing to wear. So we kept a sharp eye out as the bus rumbled past St. Rita's Church and convent. And even as we automatically made the sign of the cross, because we were passing a church, we watched for nuns waiting at the bus stop there. If we spotted a pair of them, we'd arrange our beach towels modestly over our skinny bare thighs, and chorus, "Afternoon, Sister" as they whisked past our seat, with a flick of black veil.

Nuns. Never, in all my years of grade school, had I a teacher who was not a nun. During the school year, I alternately feared and worshiped them. They defined the perimeters of my life, punctuated its high points with approval or disapproval, dictated what I would wear, and ruled on what behavior was acceptable and what might send my immortal soul to hell. They were all nine feet tall and they were all omnipotent. It rather surprised me that the person selected for pope was some tottering old man. A strapping young nun could certainly have done the job better. I harbored no doubts about which was the superior sex: Nuns were.

But in summer, deprived of their captives, the nuns entered a temporary period of relative helplessness, like crabs when they molt. Despite the heat—air conditioning hadn't spread throughout the middle-class world yet—the nuns weren't allowed to shed. They must have been terribly hot, in their bulky black habits, heads rigid in starched linen.

Twenty years later, my friend Sister Helen Prejean would confirm that yes, they did perspire; they perspired a lot, under those many layers of cloth. But they never showed it, beyond a little brow-patting with a plain white handkerchief pulled from the endless folds of a long skirt. They kept up with the mobs of sweaty kids at summer camps (a nun in full habit taught me to bait a fishhook at the old Camp St. Joseph in Bay St. Louis, Mississippi) and slogged through hours overseeing the unfortunates in summer school, all the while appearing crisp and cool, smelling of Ivory soap.

I didn't know it then, and wouldn't have believed it anyway, but some nuns actually got to go swimming, in private camps their orders rented on Lake Ponchartrain. And therein lies a tale. Some youngish nuns from a New Orleans convent had donned modest bathing suits and slipped into the lake behind their camp. For safety's sake, they had a lifeguard—a young priest. Of course he wouldn't dream of watching nuns frolic in the water. So he stood in front of the camp, out of sight but within earshot. And then he heard screams. One Sister had drifted out too far and couldn't make it back to shore.

He swam to the rescue, but when he actually got within reach of her, he hesitated. How do you properly get hold of a nun? There was no class on that in the seminary. A leg was kicking his way, but surely he couldn't touch a nun's leg. And it would hardly be appropriate to clutch her in a chest carry. The Sister, naturally, knew what he was thinking. But, being a nun, she was the soul of practicality. She was also desperate. "Grab me, Father," she yelled. "Grab me anywhere!"

I heard that story from Sister Helen. While nuns had been my mentors all my life, and some of my friends became nuns, she was the first nun I met who then became a friend.

I'd read about Sister Helen before I met her in 1985. I was a freelance writer, and she was a story. She'd made news by standing up for a convicted rapist and murder, Pat Sonnier, opposing his execution—although anyone with a lick of sense would know he richly deserved execution, I thought. I firmly believed in the death penalty. Hadn't Sister Emmanuel said, back in third grade, that when you kill someone you give up your right to life?

I talked the editor of *The Clarion-Herald*, the New Orleans Catholic newspaper, into letting me do a story on this obviously misguided Sister Helen. She said she would be happy to talk to me, if I would meet her where she lived and worked—in the St. Thomas Housing Project.

That was the last place I wanted to go. I lived in the suburbs with my husband and children, and my specialty was humorous little features, or young mothers' stories like "How to Make a Christmas Creche with Your Child"—that sort of thing. Talking to a nun I could handle. Meeting her in an infamous inner-city project—I wasn't so sure.

But I gritted my teeth and met her anyway, on the wide porch of Hope House, a green-and-white house nestled next to the project's dingy brick walls. Hope House would one day appear in the movie *Dead Man Walking*, based on the book that Helen would write. But neither of us knew that yet.

She wasn't nine feet tall—close to five-foot-four, and she wore slacks and a pretty flowered shirt under a mop of dark hair. We introduced ourselves and made pleasant small talk. She asked if I had kids. I said I had six, and braced myself for the inevitable, "Bless you, child!" It didn't come, and that was a relief. We went on to other things. She said something that made me laugh, and I said something that made her laugh, and then we were friends. We discovered we were close to the same age, and had similar Catholic backgrounds.

I took out my notepad. "Tell me about Patrick Sonnier."

"Okay," she said. "I'm just going to tell you what happened, and I know you'll do a good job with it."

Well. Most people who promote a cause tell you exactly what they want you to say, and how to say it. This was different.

An office of the Louisiana Coalition of Jails and Prisons was just around the corner on Magazine Street, Helen said. A staff member asked her if she would become a pen pal to someone on death row. "They are often forgotten. They don't get much mail," she told Helen.

And so began a correspondence, which blossomed into a friendship and ended in a crusade. Pat Sonnier had been convicted, along with his brother Eddie, in the murder of two teenagers in a cane field near St. Martinville. After Pat was sentenced to death, Eddie came forward and said he was the one who actually pulled the trigger. But the court didn't buy that, and Pat was executed. Helen believed Eddie and fought fiercely to stop Pat's execution, which shocked conservative Catholics, such as me.

She lost the battle, and Sonnier died. His family had no money for a burial plot, so she arranged for him to be buried in a section of a Baton Rouge cemetery reserved for nuns. The nuns agreed to that, but a lot of other people were offended. They wrote letters to the editor of *The Times-Picayune*. One letter, which she relished, called her, "Sister Jane Fonda." Some insinuated that the poor little nun must have fallen in love with the criminal.

"No," she said, "I didn't even want him to be let out of prison. In no way do I condone what they did."

Helen was one of three children of Louis and Gusta Mae Prejean of Baton Rouge, Louisiana, who were not only loving parents, but religious. "We'd say a family rosary every night and my parents would ask God for more vocations to the church—and that one of their children would be granted a vocation."

She went to St. Joseph Academy in Baton Rouge. A doer and a shaker even then, she was president of her senior class. After graduation in 1957, she went straight to the novitiate of the St. Joseph Sisters on Mirabeau Avenue in New Orleans. God had answered the Prejeans' prayers.

That was when nuns still acted like nuns, appearing in public two-by-two, wearing long black habits, hands tucked into their sleeves, rosaries clicking at their sides. Prejean stopped being Helen and became Sister Louis Augustine. She took vows of poverty, chastity, and obedience, and she was taught to be humble and quiet. "It wasn't the way to develop leadership qualities. But it made you appreciate solitude and peacefulness. It gave you interiority—not to live for external things, but to find rewards within yourself."

She also learned to get up at 5 A.M. for prayers and to observe "sacred silence" after 9:30 P.M.—a very scheduled routine, not unlike that of her future friends at Angola State Penitentiary.

With other young Sisters, Helen attended classes at St. Mary's Dominican College, took a bachelor's degree in education, then taught seventh and eighth grades at St. Frances Cabrini, a parochial school in the suburbs.

"Once, I set my veil on fire when I was lighting an Advent wreath. I was trying to lead the class in prayer and the kids were all screaming, 'Sister! Sister! You're on fire!'"

She got through the experience unscathed. And if things hadn't changed, Sister Louis Augustine might have bustled through a life devoted to grade-schoolers, never being accused of cozying up to convicted murderers.

But a force that would reshape the age-old ways of her faith and her life was being born at the Second Vatican Council in Rome. In 1966, the Sisters of St. Joseph dispatched the ever-enthusiastic Sister Louis Augustine to Canada to get a master's degree in religious education, in keeping with this new brand of Catholicism. When she came back, she stopped being Sister Louis Augustine and became Helen again. Sister Helen. She put away her habit and turned her attention to works other than teaching: parish ministry and novice mistress.

Then, in 1980, she heard Harvard sociologist Sister Marie Augusta Neal speak at a Sisters' conference in Terre Haute, Indiana. Neal insisted that to follow Christ meant to embrace the poor and work for justice.

Helen couldn't get that out of her mind. She reflected, prayed about it, and finally asked and was granted permission to move into the St. Thomas Housing Project with other nuns. She began work at Hope House.

I wrote all this in the story for *The Clarion-Herald*, but realized it didn't even scratch the surface of what Sister Helen was all about. And although I wasn't yet convinced by her arguments against the death penalty, I was interested. So I proposed a longer story about her to *New Orleans Magazine*, a glossy publication that makes a point of covering much more than the city's tourist attractions.

The editor liked the idea, but told me I'd have to go to Louisiana's death row and interview Robert Lee Willie, the condemned man Helen was currently visiting. That gave me pause. His was a gruesome story; he had kidnapped, maimed, and raped. He had admitted killing once; he may have killed more than once. I didn't relish the idea of talking to him. But, I'd come this far.

Helen and I drove to the prison together. We decided that she would sit down with him, and then I would. I watched the guards frisk her before she went in. She wasn't allowed to carry so much as a pencil. When my turn came, I walked in with my briefcase. No search required.

"Sister Helen—I trust her. Like my mother." Willie told me. "I know that she really cares. I never was a religious man, but she has helped me. I can find…" he struggled for words, "I have found the truth in myself."

He was thoughtful now that he was in shackles, free of drugs and alcohol. Helen did not think he should be free, but that he could function in prison. And, she pointed out, an execution costs more than life imprisonment.

But I couldn't stop envisioning what he'd done. After my two-hour interview, I found Helen waiting. "I need to call home," I told her. "I'm scared. Maybe something has happened to my kids." I actually was fighting panic.

"What you're feeling is normal," Helen reassured me. "When you're confronted with something like this, all your emotions come into play." She drove me to a pay phone anyway. I called, and they were all fine.

That story won an award from the Press Club of New Orleans, and I had thoughts about going on to do a book. That was fine with Helen. "I do a little writing myself," she said. Then she showed me what she'd written. Not only was she an inspired writer, but she'd kept a journal. If a book came out of this, she was the one to write it. I told her so, and two reporters from *The New Orleans Times-Picayune,* Jim Hodge and Jason DeParle, told her the same thing.

As it happened, she landed a contract with Random House for *Dead Man Walking* at the same time I landed one with St. Martin's Press for my humor book, *Never Heave Your Bosom In a Front Hook Bra,* a compilation of columns I had written for *New Orleans Magazine.* We flew to

New York together, to meet our New York editors. Coming home, we celebrated with an airline bottle of Scotch for her, and white wine for me.

By then, I had absorbed, via Helen, so much about the death penalty that, despite Sister Emmanuel's early teaching, I realized the state had no right to kill people—especially given that the state seemed to get it wrong so often, as Helen illustrated in her second book, *The Death of Innocents: An Eyewitness Account of Wrongful Executions*. I helped edit that one, served as her press agent a few times, went along as her sidekick on various adventures, and on one unforgettable occasion, slept alongside her on the floor of a homeless shelter.

And I learned a lot. One thing was never to let her make the travel arrangements (see above on homeless shelter).

And, by osmosis, I absorbed her views of how the world should be. Nothing really new—the same things that other nuns had preached to me all my life. But she was actually doing them. Love your neighbor, even those who are different from you. Pray for the less fortunate, then roll up your sleeves and help them. And insist that your government play fair.

I don't ride the bus and watch for nuns anymore. But I still think one should be pope.

Liz Scott Monaghan is an award-winning columnist and contributing editor for New Orleans Magazine. *She has been an instructor of journalism and adviser to the student media at Loyola University, New Orleans, and is the author of humor books, including her newest,* Never Clean Your House During Hurricane Season. *Monaghan wrote this essay as Hurricane Isaac was bearing down on her home.*

Blessed are the Sisters (as They Are the Real Deal)

Adriana Trigiani

When I was six years old, Sister Theresa Kelly of the Salesian Sisters of St. Don Bosco was a movie star to me. She was beautiful, graceful, and wore a black habit with a full skirt and billowing sleeves.

In the late 1960s, the outside world was in tumult. But within the walls of Our Lady of Mount Carmel School in Roseto, Pennsylvania, the Salesians were still wearing their habits, large crosses, and veils. They ran the school and lived in a traditional community in the building that housed the kindergarten classroom.

I came up as a Catholic girl after Vatican II, and just as quickly as the Holy Ghost was renamed Holy Spirit, the Sisters began to change. The role of nuns, their approach to their work, and even their names began to evolve in the dawn of women's liberation. The nuns were doing the heavy lifting, and everyone knew it.

When our family moved to Big Stone Gap, Virginia, it was an adventure and a culture shock. We went from a place where it seemed everyone was Catholic, to a place where it seemed few were. We joined Sacred Heart Church in Appalachia, and our priest was Father John Otterbacher, a Glenmary Home Missioner. We also met the Glenmary Sisters, who were already wearing short habits and only wore their veils during Mass. Father Otterbacher wore a plaid flannel work shirt when he stopped by to meet us for the first time. Without a Roman collar, he looked like everyone else. I soon grew to understand that when it came to the Glenmarys, that was the point.

The Glenmary nuns were a thoughtful, young, energetic group led by Mother Superior Catherine Rumschlag. Besides their work in the community, helping families of different faiths or none, they taught Sunday School, assisted at Mass, led the music, and took a keen interest in the children.

Some of my first artistic projects, including making slides and setting the images to music, were encouraged by the Sisters. They had simple names, like Ann and Monica. Without the long skirts and veils, they were accessible, it seemed, and modern. They were also devoted, hard-working, and fiercely independent. They were in service to the people of Appalachia, and, as the boots on the ground (or in their case, sensible shoes), they decided how they would lead their mission.

If you read the book *Mountain Sisters: From Convent to Community in Appalachia,* the true story of their order as told by the Sisters them-selves, you will find a history of their commitment in Appalachia as they worked and learned, shared and coped, and eventually dissolved to form a different community to serve the people of the mountains.

I remember, from when I was a girl, the transformation of the nuns in habits to working women of faith. I don't remember a ruckus, but I do remember an insistence by the Sisters to lead forth in their own way. Many still came to Mass, but transitioned into the work world. Sister Catherine ran the cooperative Bread and Chicken House in Big Stone Gap. As a nun, she worked long hours, and as a layperson, she worked longer hours.

At each critical point in my growth as a person of faith, I have turned to the Sisters. In nearby Norton, Virginia, the Poor Servants of God, led by Sister Ann Christine, put down roots and formed St. Mary's Hospital, where most of my friends were born. The nuns began the St. Mary's Health Wagon, operated by Sister Bernadette Kenny—who is considered a saint back home—as she brought medicine and supplies to families high in the mountains and in the hollers where there were no doctors and little hope. [Editor's note: For more on Sister Bernadette Kenny and the Health Wagon, see the next chapter, "Mountain Health Care on Wheels."]

The Salesians, Glenmarys, and Poor Servants of God shaped my girlhood, while the Sisters of St. Joseph at Saint Mary's College in Notre Dame, Indiana, fed my intellect and challenged my artistic sensibilities as a young adult. Sister Jean Klene encouraged my approach to playwriting and directing in the theater as a Shakespeare scholar with a keen mind and fabulous sense of humor. Sister Karol Jackowski, a total original and a published author of wonderful books, has been a steadfast friend and inspiration since my days in Regina Hall.

When it came time to find a school for our daughter, Lucia, we looked to the Sisters again, finding the Religious of the Sacred Heart of Jesus, founded by St. Madeleine Sophie Barat, as a place where we knew our daughter would be nurtured. The Sisters, regardless of order, have always been there for me, and now, too, for my daughter.

My daughter sees what I have observed all my life. Women multitask, sacrifice, and invent their own ways to change the world, one small act at a time. They work around impenetrable walls, and find new ways to achieve their goals in the face of resistance. When a Sister cannot go through, she goes around.

Women nurture, support, and lead. They question, rise up, lose, and fail, only to come back stronger for the fight. The Sisters are relentless workers in the causes of social justice; their ministry has no limits, their reach, no borders. They know more than we give them credit for and, despite our lack of gratitude, they serve with gusto without expectation of praise or reward. There is no golden staff or puff of smoke to acknowledge their ascent, only the quiet knowledge that they are easing the burden of another woman's daily struggle as she raises a family in the light of God's love.

It never dawned on me that the voices of the nuns should carry less weight or that their commitment to the salvation of my soul was any less important than the commitment of the village priest's or the diocesan bishop's. It seemed to me, both then and now, that the Sisters are the engine of faith in the Holy Roman Church, and without them, we would not be a community at all. As women have done since the beginning of time, they take the resources at hand and make a home. Sisters around the world provide education, shelter, and health care. Like good mothers, they live to serve us without any expectation of reciprocity.

The Sisters carry on their work, steadfastly and often quietly, knowing that the job that needs to be done is more important than the crowing it takes to draw attention to it. The Sisters are so good at what they do; we hardly notice them. They move through the world stealthily, with purpose, their mission clear, their workload without end.

And somehow, knowing all they have done, and all that lies ahead to do, they have somehow found the time to make us all a family. I remain one grateful daughter.

Adriana Trigiani is a screenwriter, producer, film director, and novelist. In 1996, she won the Most Popular Documentary award at the Hamptons International Film Festival for directing Queens of the Big Time. *The next year, she coproduced the documentary* Green Chimneys. *In 2001, Trigiani wrote a novel,* Big Stone Gap, *based on her hometown and her screenplay by the same name. Her latest novel is the bestselling* The Shoemaker's Wife.

Mountain Health Care on Wheels

FR. JOHN S. RAUSCH

Teresa Gardner changes the oil on the Health Wagon every three thousand miles. This thirty-foot Winnebago outfitted as a mobile medical clinic sits in the parking lot of her office when I arrive in Wise, Virginia, to interview her about her work.

Since 1988 Teresa has embraced the Health Wagon as her life's work, encouraged by the potential good she can do for her neighbors and inspired by the woman who began the clinic, Sister Bernadette Kenny. Working alongside Sister Bernie, Teresa gained the skills and confidence to make a difference in this Appalachian mountain region. Cracking a smile when talking about her, Teresa fondly adds, "She's also my hero."

Teresa oversees two such mobile clinics that travel rough rural roads to remote towns and coal camps in four Southwest Virginia counties. In addition, there are two stationary offices: one in Clintwood, and a new, 4,900-square-foot specialty clinic located near the Wise campus of the University of Virginia, whose students and faculty enjoy a working relationship with the Health Wagon staff. Combined, the clinics have six exam rooms and a dental office, but no full-time doctor.

All told, between the two stationary facilities and the two mobile clinics, nurse practitioners, LPNs, and other health-care professionals treat nearly four thousand patients annually. The whole health-care program runs on a modest budget, funded in part by an endowment from the Catholic Diocese of Richmond and numerous private donations.

The Health Wagon rolls into the communities of patients in Dickenson, Wise, Russell, and Buchanan counties either weekly or in alternate weeks, and provides their only safety net for health care. "We have to be innovative," Teresa reflects. "We're using our own assessment skills rather than ordering all the tests that these patients can't afford anyway."

When I asked about her dreams as a child, her story sounded not too different from the calling of a Sister or other vowed religious in the Catholic tradition: "My mother's unfulfilled ambition was to be a missionary overseas, and I feel I inherited that. I wanted to be a doctor growing up and always loved helping people. I would get medical books and read them when I was a child."

Teresa was born at St. Mary's Hospital in Norton, and she knew the dedication of the Poor Servants of the Mother of God, an Irish community of Sisters who ran the hospital. She nurtured a deep respect for them, but when she became the first employee of the Health Wagon and a close associate of Sister Bernie's, she found a kindred spirit who inspired her.

"I met her at the hospital for the job interview and loved her since that first meeting," Teresa says. "She was very kind and not really what I thought a nun might be. She did not wear her habit as traditionally they had done at St. Mary's Hospital."

As they worked together, Sister Bernie gently nudged Teresa to pursue the master's degree required for a family nurse practitioner (NP). "I knew right away that I would like to become an NP like Sister Bernie," she reflects. "Definitely she ignited this passion in my life. She was inspiring on a daily basis with what she was accomplishing in health care here in the Appalachian Mountains."

Over the years and over the miles, she assisted Sister Bernie with dedication as they treated the prevalent illnesses of the mountains: diabetes, obesity, heart problems, and chronic obstructive pulmonary diseases (COPDs) such as emphysema and chronic bronchitis. Years later, because of her relentless work with the Health Wagon and rural medicine, Teresa was honored by the American Academy of Nurse Practitioners with their 2012 Domestic Humanitarian Award.

When Sister Bernie entered semiretirement in 2005, Teresa succeeded her as director of the Health Wagon and all its programs. In her mind, she was assuming the mantle of a pioneer: "Sister Bernie was ahead of her time, doing thirty years ago what we in health care are now pushing."

Sister Bernie

In 1978, at the invitation of Bishop Walter Sullivan of Richmond, Sister Bernie came to work in Dickenson County because there was no hospital in that area. Her community, the Medical Missionaries of Mary, seized this opportunity as a way to serve a pocket of poverty in America while preparing their Sister candidates for work in Africa.

Many Sisters, especially those freed from their teaching responsibilities in the 1970s and 1980s because Catholic schools were hiring more lay teachers, saw Appalachia as a unique opportunity to serve the poor and stand with the oppressed. Indeed, numerous women religious from across the country came to the mountains to serve in ministry because the Appalachian bishops had said, "In the contemporary mission of the Church, the voice and action of women bring a special charism to the struggle for justice."

With all the compassionate ministries the Sisters did, none was more appreciated by folks in the hollows than basic health care.

The concept for the Health Wagon began in 1980 when Sister Bernie grabbed her medical bag and jumped into her VW Beetle to visit area residents who were sick. Driving to the patients "ensures that folks get health care," she says. "The advantage of going to the people shows that you really care."

For three years the light blue Beetle traveled the hollows and ridges around Dickenson County so Sister Bernie could take blood pressure, check for diabetes, and dispense proper medications. She bought her VW used for $500 with over 100,000 miles on it, and retired it with just under 300,000!

In 1983 after Bishop Walter Sullivan donated the Health Wagon to Sister Bernie for her work (actually, he sold it to her for one dollar), St. Mary's Hospital agreed to sponsor the clinic for accreditation so she could address the pressing medical needs of the area. Data showed that about one-third of the target population was obese. Rates of heart disease, diabetes, and cancer were higher than the national average, as were death rates from lung, cervical, and colorectal cancers.

To access medical services, residents also faced social and economic barriers, such as limited public transportation, lack of health insurance, out-of-pocket costs, and shortages of health-care professionals. Thus, the Health Wagon readily took on as its mission a mandate to serve "the healthcare needs of the uninsured, underinsured, and disenfranchised in the mountains of Appalachia in Southwest Virginia."

In the mountains, word travels quickly and everywhere when there is a need: Folks learn who to call. One wintry night Sister Bernie answered a call from a woman in labor who lived near the head of the hollow, the farthest point in. With her medical kit beside her she drove the icy roads to the woman's house as far as she could, then walked the last half-mile in the dark to find her. The two held on to one another like dancers as they gingerly walked down the creek bed back to the car. Miraculously, she got the woman to the hospital just minutes before the healthy baby arrived. Word spread even wider that Sister Bernie literally went the extra mile to help someone.

On another occasion, a twenty-seven-year-old man staggered onto the Health Wagon with one eye shut and his jaw severely swollen from two abscessed teeth. He had had the toothache for two weeks, but, without health insurance, had decided on home remedies. He tried aspirin, then whiskey, then lukewarm saltwater. The pain persisted.

Finally he remembered that his granddaddy applied WD-40 lubricant to his knee and other joints and somehow that seemed to help. So, in desperation, he applied WD-40 directly to the nerve to kill the pain. When Sister Bernie heard his story, she panicked, knowing the toxic substance could travel directly to the brain. She administered antibiotics immediately to counter the infection. Then, using her grandmotherly charm, she phoned the only nearby dentist, devised a favorable payment plan, and cajoled him into pulling the teeth.

When I remind Teresa about some of the stories Sister Bernie told me, her reaction lacks surprise. "Bernie is Bernie—she's so admirable," Teresa smiles at the tooth story. "By hook or by crook she would get it for people."

In 1998 Sister Bernie; Teresa; JoElla Dales, LPN; Stan Brock; and Tony Roberts from the Norton Lion's Club began planning the first area-wide clinic at the Wise County Fair Grounds. The next year they began offering the most-needed services in the mountains: dental and vision care. Every year since the event has grown, spearheaded by the Health Wagon with the support of the local community and of Remote Area Medical (RAM), an international program. Patients camp out the night before to ensure their place for medical treatment.

In 2010 the Wise RAM Clinic surpassed the U.S. record for the number of patients seen in one three-day period: 6,869. Of that number, over 4,000 patient encounters concerned general medical procedures, nearly 1,000 were eye exams and fittings for glasses, and another 1,400 dealt with general dentistry; technicians also provided 207 mammograms. All told, the 2010 RAM contributed $2.3 million of free health care, with 1,898 volunteers mostly from the medical profession donating over 20,000 hours of service.

Sister Bernie's experience spans a vast mission field, from her early experiences in Africa to her years in Appalachia, so it was not unusual that she would become a resource to students preparing for rural ministry.

The Appalachian Ministries Educational Resource Center (AMERC), located in Berea, Kentucky, a few hours away, consistently sends students to meet her. She receives them with homemade cake or cookies while sharing her stories with humility and openness. Students learn that chronic illnesses like diabetes, hypertension, high cholesterol, depression, and heart disease abound in Appalachia, that large numbers of people there lack health insurance, and that their health is related to their nutrition, environment, job security, and spiritual well-being. Without this understanding, health care in the mountains would only treat symptoms and the ministry would lack the authentic compassion of Christ.

I once brought a group of seminarians to visit the Health Wagon at around two o'clock in the afternoon, when Sister Bernie had already seen thirty-four patients since early morning. She pointed to two sacks of vegetables as her total revenue for the day, and noted that people contributed what they could but that occasionally times grew lean.

Still, Teresa said, "Bernie and I ate good: pies, cakes, jellies, jams, vegetables—anything folks could bring out of their fridge. Part was in payment, but some was a contribution." Sister Bernie understands how sharing builds relationships that form the core of a therapeutic community.

While my students would be fascinated with stories of the remote travels of the Health Wagon, I had to ask Sister Bernie about her arrest with the seminarians, because the story has become an iconic tale of power and struggle in the mountains.

When the Pittston Coal Company canceled health coverage for retired miners back in 1989, the United Mine Workers of America went on strike. Pittston was swept along with the growing trend to raise profits by cutting benefits, but the miners affected most were the retired fathers and uncles of Pittston's current workforce, many of whom had black lung from working in the mines. The strike lingered several months and grew so bitter that fully a fourth of the entire Virginia State Police force came to Russell and Dickenson counties.

One of the drivers, Tracy, remembers steering the Health Wagon slowly as it made its way through the coal town of Trammel during the strike, when Sister Bernie pointed out a box in the middle of the road. She cautioned, "Watch out! Watch out! Go around that box."

Bernie explained that a common weapon used to stop trucks from hauling coal during the strike, "was called a jackrock, which consisted of two ten-penny nails bent at right angles and welded together. Whenever a jackrock is thrown, it will always land with one sharp spike sticking up, guaranteeing a puncture even to a large truck tire that runs over it." Boxes such as the one they saw in the road were often used to conceal a jackrock.

As the strike wore on, the area seemed almost as if it were an occupied war zone. Hundreds of state police officers were everywhere; arrests were constant, especially for the practice of driving slowly—a strike tactic to slow down the flow of coal being mined and transported by nonunion labor.

Sister Bernie steadfastly made her rounds, tending to her patients scattered throughout five mountain communities. One day as the Winnebago crawled along like a racing turtle, Sister Bernie momentarily stopped in front of the Binns-Counts Community Center in Stratton and, out of the driver's window, handed some medicine to a patient. Since she stopped on the road itself—not an uncommon occurrence on rural roads with no shoulders—a state policeman interpreted her gesture as a deliberate attempt to impede the flow of coal and arrested her.

Sister Bernie chuckles when she recalls how a well-intentioned striker approached the officer with true mountain logic and told him, "You can't arrest her. Her husband's not home." But, arrested she was. For the next three hours she sat on the arrest bus with twenty male strikers and no restroom. Finally she convinced an officer she had to relieve herself. So, escorted by an officer with rifle, Sister Bernie ducked briefly behind a tree.

Her accommodations did not improve much at their destination. Once booked at the Washington County Jail in Abingdon, Sister Bernie became the seventh prisoner in a five-person cell. Her mattress stretched under the commode. With round-the-clock lighting and incessant talking, sleep seemed near impossible. Fortunately, her ordeal ended by 1:30 A.M., when Bishop Sullivan contacted the governor, who arranged for her release.

Years later, in 1998, Sister Bernie Kenny won the Lumen Christi (Light of Christ) Award, which the Catholic Extension Society gives to people "who are quietly doing exemplary evangelization work around the United States." At the ceremony held in the coal town of Clinchco, Bishop Sullivan recalled Sister Bernie's experience with the Pittston Strike. A front-page newspaper photo of Sister Bernie's arrest, as she was led off in handcuffs, had infuriated readers throughout the region because "the Angel of the Mountains" had been arrested. In his talk, Bishop Sullivan referred to the photo and said it was a public-relations disaster for Pittston, and a key factor in ending the strike.

The authentic role of a mentor comes with helping people see the difference between the possible and the unreal. For example, the distinction between healing and curing can get lost in the high-tech world of medicine. Medical science can see death as the enemy and sickness as a weakness. To Sister Bernie, a true mentor, illness represents a teaching moment about our humanity. She cannot cure cancer, but she can help heal the spirit.

The atmosphere she created with the Health Wagon promotes the values of caring and compassion. Patients mingle among friends, they laugh together, they hug, and they affirm one another with a gentle word or touch. Her holistic nursing approach emphasized "the therapeutic use of self"—combining stress reduction, self-care, and spirituality. Though the Health Wagon offers limited medical technology, its role in the practice of healing has deepened the meaning of each patient's life.

Teresa Gardner continues to practice the healing arts through the holistic medicine she learned on the Health Wagon. The days grow long, but she feels the "passion and desire to deliver health care to the less fortunate. I think I inherited what Sister Bernie had. God must have placed Sister Bernie here, because she just fit right in."

After all, on the Health Wagon, she adds, "We've seen miracles on a daily basis."

Fr. John S. Rausch, a Glenmary priest, writes and pursues social ministry from his home in Stanton, Kentucky. Currently he directs the Catholic Committee of Appalachia, where he has worked for over thirty-five years. In 2007 Fr. Rausch won the Teacher of Peace award from Pax Christi, USA.

Sisters' Gentleness of Spirit: An Interview With James Martin, SJ

JUDY BALL

James Martin is a Jesuit priest best known as a popular author, magazine editor, and, perhaps most widely, as the "chaplain" of Comedy Central's satirical show, *The Colbert Report*. His personal story is one of development from business manager to African missionary, to priest and communicator, shepherded by the inspiration of Sisters along the way.

Jim was raised in an Irish-Italian Catholic family in the Philadelphia suburb of Plymouth Meeting, and attended public schools all the way through college. His early religious education consisted only of religious education classes in his local parish. That was where he encountered Sister Margaret Jude, SSJ, a Sister of St. Joseph of Chestnut Hill, Pennsylvania.

He remembers being "very impressed" with the woman, still in full habit "and swathed in acres and acres of black and white." He also remembers the "great big O" she made on the blackboard as she introduced the first words of the Act of Contrition ("O my God…") in preparation for her students' upcoming First Holy Communion. From her he learned the proper way to fold his hands in prayer and march up the church aisle to receive Communion, just like the Catholic school kids.

It was the late 1960s, and the Second Vatican Council had ended a few years earlier. Sister Margaret Jude did her best to introduce the bright young boy to the tenets and traditions of the faith and prepare him for life as a Catholic. Forty or so years later the two would meet again when Father Jim was speaking at a church near his hometown, and she was a member of the audience. Sister Margaret Jude was "still going strong," he recalls.

Meanwhile, her former pupil, who joined the Jesuits in 1988 and was ordained a priest in 1999, has become a popular author and editor. Most days he can be found at *America* magazine in New York, where he serves as contributing editor.

If he's not there writing or blogging or tweeting or participating in meetings, it may be because he's working on a new book (he's written or edited more than ten) or serving as a commentator for CNN, NPR, Fox News, or Vatican Radio. (His book *The Jesuit Guide to (Almost) Everything* was a *New York Times* bestseller and, like his books *My Life with the Saints* and *Between Heaven and Mirth*, an award-winner.) Or perhaps he's preparing a homily or gathering his thoughts for an upcoming retreat he's giving. Then again, he might be getting ready to appear on Catholic comedian Stephen Colbert's show to tackle—ever so humorously—serious questions about the faith they share.

No question, Father Jim Martin is fully engaged in using whatever twenty-first–century tools he can to spread the good news. Sister Margaret Jude's former pupil is going pretty strong himself.

Q: *Many of us first experienced Sisters in Catholic elementary school classrooms, Monday to Friday for eight years. But your exposure was limited. Can you recall some of your early encounters with women religious as an adult?*

A: I had zero experience with Sisters from my C.C.D. [Sunday school] years all the way up until I entered the Jesuits at age twenty-seven. By then I had graduated from the University of Pennsylvania's Wharton School of Business and had worked in corporate finance at General Electric for six years. The first woman religious I met (since elementary school, that is) was when I was in the Jesuit novitiate. A Dominican Sister came to speak to us novices about her work as a prison minister. I was so impressed!

Over time I met more and more Sisters who were doing retreat ministry, working in local parishes, were friends of the Jesuits with whom I lived, or who were fellow retreatants during my annual retreats. Gradually, they became a part of my world.

Q: *What roles have women religious played in your life since you entered religious life in 1988?*

A: In my time as a Jesuit I've become good friends with a great many women religious. Many of them are my heroes as mentors, teachers, spiritual directors, counselors, coworkers, and friends. In them I see people who have given up everything for Christ. Overall, they lack what you might call "institutional power" in the Church—typically, they don't have official roles in the Church's hierarchical structure—but they do their work with a great deal of joy and vivacity and faith.

Frankly, women religious have been some of the most influential people in my entire life. They have influenced me by being not only friends and companions in the Lord but also role models. They are not just peers. They are also people I look up to.

Q: *Are there specific ways they have inspired you?*

A: The main way is by showing how much they are able to do with so little. These women are of course not ordained; they don't run Vatican congregations; they don't run dioceses or archdioceses; they don't run parishes. As women who live a vow of poverty, they also don't have much money. And they often minister behind the scenes in low-paying jobs, say, as elementary school teachers or spiritual directors or pastoral associates. For the most part, they're not making headlines or earning great ecclesial honors. These women are—on the face of it—powerless. To be able to minister in such a situation, and to flourish, is astonishing. They are able to do much in the Church through their work for God.

Q: *So they are both powerless and powerful?*

A: Exactly. Sisters don't fill hierarchical roles in the Church, but they have the power of the Gospel. They have the power of their relationship with Christ. They may not have a great deal of institutional power but they have a great deal of power among the people of God.

Sisters are—and should be—enormously respected. Just ask Catholics about the women religious in their parishes, or about the Sisters who taught them in school, served as their spiritual director, or were the hospital chaplain when someone in their family was sick. They'll speak in glowing terms about these women. There's a kind of moral or spiritual power they have that makes up for their lack of institutional power.

Q: *Do you feel your approach to life or your work is influenced by women religious?*

A: Oh, yes, but it's a little hard to sort out just how. In my experience, Sisters have a certain way of being in the world. It's very gentle, hopeful, loving, and sometimes playful. They have a gentle way of being. Now, I don't always achieve that myself. In fact, it may not be something you can say is ever "achieved." But it's something I aspire to. Whenever I'm around women religious I experience a feeling of gentleness that is very hard to define or describe. I'm sure other people recognize it.

I try to bring that into my own life, although it's difficult. Maybe it has something to do with feminine energy—even though that may sound stereotypical. Perhaps men, like me, are more aggressive. Or perhaps it's due to their formation or their position of institutional powerlessness and the freedom that comes with that. Or perhaps it's due to their contact with the poor and marginalized. Who knows? Though it's hard for me to define it, there is something special about the personality, if you will, of the woman religious. Not that they're all the same—far from it! But there is definitely a gentleness of spirit that I so appreciate—and seek to emulate.

Q: *Let's talk about some of the women religious who, as you've said, are your "heroes" and "role models" for various reasons. Who comes to mind?*

A: One of the Sisters I'm closest to is Janice Farnham, a Religious of Jesus and Mary. She was my professor of Church history at the Weston Jesuit School of Theology in Cambridge, Massachusetts, when I was in the midst of my Jesuit formation. Janice was a terrific teacher who, over time, became friends with me and with my parents. She met them during my diaconate ordination in 1998, and could not have been more friendly or welcoming to them. My parents liked her immediately. "She's a great lady," my dad would often say.

When I shared the news with her that my father had been diagnosed with cancer, she was on the phone with him in just a few hours. And toward the end of his life, when he was in hospice care, Janice got on a train from Boston, rode six hours to Philadelphia, found a place to stay overnight at a nearby convent, visited my father in the hospice for an hour or two—and then got back on the train the next day and returned to Boston. Isn't that incredible? It was one of the kindest things anyone has ever done for me.

Sister Janice also gave me two beautiful pieces of advice as my father approached death. First, when I mentioned to her that he was talking about God and Jesus in a way he never had, she reminded me that death is about "becoming more human," that as we die we become more open, more vulnerable. "He's becoming more himself," she said. It was so helpful to me to hear this.

And earlier, when I told her how frightened I was about helping care for my dad and helping to accompany him (and my mother) on his path to death, she gently asked, "Can you surrender to the future that God has in store for you?" I thought that was so beautiful. I use those words all the time with people now, and I underline that that wisdom, which helped change the way I see suffering, came from a woman religious.

Q: *What other Sisters come to mind?*
A: I'd like to talk about several women religious who profoundly touched my life when I was a still a seminarian and working with Jesuit Refugee Service in Nairobi, Kenya, helping refugees start small businesses. One is Sister Maddy Tiberii, a Sister of St. Joseph of Springfield, Massachusetts. We met when she and two of her Sisters were helping to run a girls' school in a small town in Tanzania called Kowak. For their vacation, the three of them would come up to Nairobi and stay at our Jesuit house in our guest rooms a few times a year.

Maddy would come—I laugh as I think of this—and relax by preparing spectacular meals for us, huge Italian meals. The perfect guest, we used to say! Maddy was always so adventuresome and energetic, so upbeat and funny, and I marveled at her zest for life in the midst of difficult circumstances. She was a real model for me of how to bring your best self to your work with the poor. She and I got to be very good friends, and in recent years we've given annual retreats together. Not only are they always fun, but her retreat talks always teach me something.

While in Nairobi I found the same joyful spirit in Sisters Clare and Eileen, two elderly Maryknollers who had been working in East Africa for years and who were, at the time, running a guest house for Maryknoll Sisters in the area. They lived right across the street from us in Nairobi. I would go over to their house frequently for a visit or a cup of tea or a meal. If I was sick, they would look after me. They were rather grandmotherly figures who were always laughing and joking and helping me put my challenges in perspective. Sometimes when I would lament some little illness, Sister Eileen would say, "Oh you'll be fine."

And I thought, "Well, if this elderly Sister can be so hopeful, so can I."

And right down the street from us were the Little Sisters of Jesus, who live extremely simply. Eight or nine of them lived in a small bungalow, and they would frequently invite me over for dinner and listen to me babble on about my work. I was always welcome, and we laughed so much together. In fact, I think it was the most joyful group of people I've ever been with, bar none. (Or bar nun, I guess.)

I also got to know a German Dominican, Sister Louise Radlmeier, who had worked with Sudanese refugees through the Jesuit Refugee Service scholarship program, which would provide school funds for refugee children living in Nairobi. She took such good care of them; she was like their mother. Everyone knew her. In fact one Sudanese boy (one of the "Lost Boys" of Sudan who traveled from their country to Kenya) told me that all he knew when he left Sudan was that he had to "find Sister Louise."

In Nairobi, I was immersed not only in Kenyan culture but also the culture of Catholic women religious. It was a huge blessing. To this day, I remain friends with them. They're just amazing! To be able to endure all that, often as middle-aged or elderly women, was just a huge inspiration. And I also can't forget the Missionaries of Charity with whom I worked as a Jesuit novice for four months, at a hospice for the sick and dying in Jamaica. I was so moved by their industry and hard work, their selflessness and their cheer.

Q: *As you think about these particular women religious—in the United States and abroad—who have had such an impact on your life, what do you consider the most important values they have taught you?*

A: The first is joy. The Sisters in Kenya were almost always laughing, living fully and joyfully. Sister Maddy, who is now back in the States, always had a smile on her face even in the midst of difficulties. Sister

Janice is the same. It's an infectious joy that says: "Sure there are problems, but we believe in the Gospel, and we believe that God is with us."

Next is humility. None of these women is particularly well-known; none of them is a household name. Each of them has done very simple work, not in the sense of "easy" but tackling jobs that do not have a great deal of status attached to them. And yet they carry out their ministry with such joy and zeal.

For a number of reasons, I have a certain degree of name recognition these days, and it's easy to get puffed up. So it's always good to be reminded what it's really about: the Gospel. Not me. And Jesus reminds us that those of us who want to be great must serve, and those who want to be first must be the slave. The Sisters know this and live this.

Finally, their lives teach me about faith. For women religious, it's always about Jesus, about the People of God. There's very little striving or ambition. During our final vows, we Jesuits take a promise not to strive for or "ambition" any high office in the Jesuits or in the Church. And I see that reflected in what the Sisters do with their lives. Their whole lives embody that kind of humility.

One of my favorite musicians, Sister Kathleen Deignan, CND, sums it up so well in a lyric from a song of hers: "Be Always Little, Humble, Poor." I'm not sure if it's a quote from her foundress or from another source, but it's something that Sisters do, and it is part of their strength. They are free of the need to control, to possess, to be on top, to be thought of as successful or powerful or influential. To paraphrase Pope John XXIII, once you renounce everything, then even the most difficult task becomes easy.

You know, I'm always amazed at how much these Sisters are able to do with such little institutional power, with such little money and often with such little respect from the public at large. I'm always reminded of the line about the actress Ginger Rogers. They said that she did everything that her dancing partner Fred Astaire did, except "backwards and in high heels."

Q: *Clearly, you continue to treasure these women who have been so important at various times and places in your life. Is that why you affirm them in your talks and books?*
A: Absolutely. I write a lot about spirituality, and much of what I've learned about that subject I've learned from women religious. And more specifically, much of what I've learned about Ignatian spirituality I've learned from women religious—on retreats in particular. And even more specifically, one summer I took a course in Ignatian spirituality and the Spiritual Exercises run by a Jesuit, Bill Creed, but also by an Ursuline nun from Louisville, Martha Buser.

Overall, I experience Sisters as joyful, friendly, sweet, loving, and caring people. They are just wonderful women. They're friends, and I love them.

I especially applaud the Sisters who wholeheartedly embraced the changes of the Second Vatican Council. Most of the women religious I know, who are now in their sixties, seventies, and eighties, were, you could say, the "fruits" of Vatican II. They entered religious life fully intending to live a traditional religious life: semi-cloistered, in a habit, doing traditional Church works.

But the documents at the time of Vatican II (like *Perfectae Caritatis* and *Evangelica Testificatio*) encouraged them to recover the charisms of their foundresses and return to their origins. And when they went back to the original writings, they discovered that, in fact, they were supposed to be out in the world, wearing the clothes of the day, working with the people, serving the poor. And so they embraced the Council documents. So anyone who critiques certain Sisters in the wake of the Second

Vatican Council for being too much "in the world" needs to remember that they were being faithful to what the Church was asking of them.

It discourages me when popular portrayals of them in the media and entertainment make them look like ninnies or idiots or out of touch. It's the opposite of my experience: After all, they've run (and sometimes founded) universities, schools, and hospitals!

Q: *These days Sisters are also facing a new challenge. They're coping with challenges, from as high as the Vatican, that their umbrella organization does not support key Catholic teachings, such as opposition to abortion and contraception. It's reopened the question of just what Sisters do. What roles do you think women religious should play in the Church?*

A: Women religious should play as much of a role in leadership as anyone else—just as priests, bishops, or men religious do. But of course they have to do so in a different way.

I see no reason why they shouldn't, for example, be running Vatican dicasteries, that is, the official "departments" in the Vatican. There's no reason, as far as I know, that says you have to be ordained to do that. Why couldn't a Sister run, for example, the Congregation for Religious? That doesn't require Holy Orders. I think we should start to think creatively about ways that women religious can legitimately exercise power within Church structures.

Most of all, I believe Sisters should continue to provide spiritual leadership. That's the most important kind of leadership anyway. It's not for me to tell them what to do (they've had enough men telling them what to do, anyway) but I believe the Sisters should continue to lead by serving, giving of themselves as Christ did. They show us the way: Be always little, humble, poor. I hope they continue to show us that simplicity and humility lead to freedom and power. And they are often ahead of the men's religious orders in this regard, because they have less to lose.

Q: *Is there anything else you'd like to say that we've not talked about?*
A: Yes there is! I would like to say to all the Sisters who are reading this: Thank you. Those two words just aren't said enough. It is impossible for me to overestimate the contributions that they have made in the Church or in my life.

I thank them personally when I can, people like Sisters Jude, Janice, Maddy, "Luise" and Martha. As for the ones who have gone before me, I hope to thank them in heaven.

....

Judy Ball is a freelance writer and editor living in Cincinnati, Ohio. She served on the staff of Franciscan Media (then St. Anthony Messenger Press) from 1996 to 2009. She was educated by Sisters of Mercy, Ursulines, and Jesuits.

Dorothy's Choice

BINKA LE BRETON

February 12, 2005. A rainy day. A trail winding through the dense forest. A woman's body huddled on the ground. Baggy Bermuda shorts, stained T-shirt, baseball cap. A cloth bag containing hand-drawn maps and a battered Bible lies next to her body while a gentle rain falls, mingling her blood with the red clay of the forest floor.

Another murder in the long history of the land wars in the Brazilian Amazon. But this time the victim is a seventy-three-year-old American Sister, Dorothy Stang. A passionate believer in social justice, Dorothy died on a red dirt road in the Amazon because she believed that every family should have access to the land they needed to feed themselves, and dared to stand up against the interests of those who wanted to destroy the last great rain forest for short-term gains.

I was traveling in Colorado when I read the newsflash about her death. I had never met Dorothy but we'd spoken on the phone. I was horrified. Like Dorothy, I live in Brazil; like Dorothy, I work in the rain forest; like Dorothy, I know that God is good. Since moving with my family from the United States to the interior of the Atlantic Forest, in Brazil, I had found a new career as a writer on environmental and human rights.

Each book had led me to examine more profoundly the problems of inequality, injustice, and exploitation. I had studied and written on the land conflicts and modern-day slavery in the Amazon, and one of my books chronicled a death foretold—the little-known case of a brave young Brazilian priest murdered twenty years before Dorothy, at a time when there were few telephones, no Internet, and nobody to know what had happened. But I'd never written about a woman, and when I heard about Dorothy I knew that I had to write her story.

It was to be one of the most profound influences on my life.

Dorothy's road to Brazil had begun seventy-three years earlier in Dayton, Ohio, where she was born the fourth of nine children to Air Force Colonel Henry Stang and his wife, Edna. Hers was a traditional Catholic upbringing where the kids went to the parish school, attended daily Mass, observed the calendar of Church festivals, and gathered each night for family prayers.

In the aftermath of the Great Depression and during the Second World War, times were hard. The kids worked around the house and in the vegetable garden, and they took summer jobs to help out. It was to be expected that the family would provide at least one vocation to the religious life, and the Stang family lived up to expectations, with two of their sons entering the priesthood and two daughters joining religious orders.

Dorothy had always had a strong streak of idealism, and a burning desire to be a missionary and do something wonderful for God. Shortly after her seventeenth birthday she joined the Sisters of Notre Dame de Namur, an extraordinary group who describe themselves as "women with hearts as wide as the world" and whose calling is to work with the poorest of the poor in the most abandoned places.

Her first venture in working with the poorest of the poor happened when she moved to Phoenix, Arizona, in 1953. She was living in a small community where the Sisters had an excellent relationship with the local priests, who encouraged the Sisters to move beyond parish work and set up programs for the children in the Mexican migrant camps and on the Navajo reservation. An article in the *Arizona Republic*, datelined December 1964, describes Dorothy (known at the time as Sister Mary Joaquim), as "a ball of fire," and talks of her wandering among "her families" in "soothing gray garb and flowing white veil, chatting one minute and dispensing discipline the next."

Ever practical, she set herself to solving the everyday problems of poverty. "Did the families need food?" the article continued, "Sister Mary found some for them. Did a family of nine living in an old bus need a place to stay? She would try to find one. Did mothers who pulled their small babies in cartons through the cotton fields as they worked need blankets and baby clothes? Sister Mary Joaquim knew there had to be some somewhere and she would find them."

These challenging and fulfilling years coincided with the lead-up to Vatican II, which formalized the movement that had been slowly evolving as some members of the Church began to reevaluate the whole concept of what it meant to live as followers of Christ. The radical new theology of liberation held that the kingdom of heaven was here and now, and that God's people were to work for social and political justice, with bias—a "preferential option"—for the poor.

It was a turbulent period as men and women sought to redefine their way of being Church, while Church authorities wrestled with the concept of relinquishing their absolute hold on power and granting increasing freedom both to those consecrated to the religious life and also to the laity who were playing an ever-more important role in the church. This new participatory way of being a Church that took its stand with the poor and powerless was both intensely exhilarating and threatening to many who were accustomed to the old paradigm.

It was in the context of this profound shake-up of old concepts and habits that Dorothy found herself moving to the country with which she was to identify herself for the rest of her life, and for whose people she was to die. There could scarcely have been a more exciting moment or place for her to embark upon her career in the mission field. Brazil was a country with a staggering difference between the lives of the rich and poor: It was one of the places where the new theology was being defined, and it was enduring the early years of an increasingly repressive military dictatorship.

It wasn't long before Dorothy found herself, true to her order, working with the poorest of the poor in one of the most abandoned places—the isolated rural settlement of Coroatá in the state of Maranhão, on the fringes of the vast Amazon forest.

Maranhão was (and is) a deeply feudal state, where both civil and religious authorities expected the nuns to run the parish schools, give catechism classes, and stay out of politics. The people of Coroatá expected the same, and had little understanding of church beyond the building where they attended Mass. But the Sisters wanted them to realize that the Church is the people of God working together to bring about God's kingdom here on earth.

Most of their parishioners lived in abject poverty. They also lived in fear—fear of the landowners, fear of the police, fear of the army. It was an intensely challenging time as the Sisters worked with the two young Italian priests to inspire people with the vision of what life could be as a Christian community of equals: following Christ in his option for the poor and the discriminated, working to bring about righteousness and peace here and now, and understanding that Christ's call to the abundant life included having access to schools, health care, and land to support their families. Dorothy had a clear vision of what the church of the poor would look like, and was determined to play her part in bringing it about.

As the government began to open up forest lands for settlement by ranchers on the one hand and smallholder farmers on the other, the dirt-poor peasants of Maranhão joined with migrants from across Brazil to stream onto the agricultural frontier. When Dorothy saw "her people" scrambling to move west, she felt called to accompany them. It was a wild and lawless frontier, where the arrival of a small band of urban idealists styling themselves guerrillas was enough to provoke the military government into establishing a massive military presence in the area.

The army immediately set about hunting down the guerrillas, and anything that smacked of the Red Peril. Suspicion naturally fell on those priests and nuns who were engaged in any form of community building. For *community*, the military commanders read "communism," and they were quick to jump on any attempts by the Church to modify its traditional support of the authorities and the status quo and identify, instead, with the peasants.

One of Dorothy's good friends, a Lutheran pastor named Marga, describes paying her a visit during this period. "She was living in a beat-up wooden building belonging to the farm workers' union. Two rooms, and the roof leaking like a sieve. Dorothy had all her things piled up on a shelf covered with plastic—papers, files, boxes of documents, a couple of changes of clothes. And there wasn't a morsel of food in the house." When Marga visited the market and later cooked supper, Dorothy took her plate and burst out laughing. It had been such a long time since she had eaten meat that she had forgotten what it tasted like.

As priests were threatened, beaten up, and expelled the Sisters found themselves increasingly taking over the role of the pastors, holding baptisms and weddings, giving Communion, anointing the sick and dying, and providing courage and comfort in the dark days.

But after an increasingly turbulent few years, during the course of which Dorothy found herself summoned to the military commander to answer for her actions, it became obvious that if she wanted to survive she would have to move out of the eye of the storm. And so it was that, in 1981, she presented herself to the bishop of Altamira, the world's largest prelacy, way out in the backlands of the Trans-Amazonian Highway. As she confided to one of the Sisters, she had always been a bit of a nomad. But this, she felt, was to be her last move.

The bishop well remembers the day she first arrived. "She turns up in Altamira," he told me when I was collecting material to write Dorothy's story. "Tells me her name is Dorothy Stang, she's an American from Ohio, a Sister of Notre Dame de Namur, and she wants to work in the Xingu region among the poorest of the poor; wants to give her life for people living in abject poverty. So I said: 'All right Dorothy. If you're looking for the poorest of the poor you'll need to go to the Trans Amazon East. It's the end of the world there. It's terrible. The people haven't got so much as a place to lay their bones.'"

Dorothy was undaunted. She set off into the back of beyond and started to work with those who had been settled by the government and then abandoned to their own devices. Their situation was desperate. There were no roads, no health service, no schools, no way they could sell any of their crops, nothing. It was the mother of all challenges, and Dorothy responded joyfully and energetically, founding schools, setting up training courses for teachers, finding technical assistance for the farmers, and helping them market what little they had to sell.

Despite his initial qualms, the bishop was impressed. "What an extraordinary woman she was," he laughed. "Oh yes, she was an activist all right! A Samaritan, in fact. Couldn't stand to see injustice and did everything she could to fight it. But deep down she was more of a prophet.

"Prophets are those who tell forth the will of God," he continued. "God's deepest desire. The prophet doesn't have a voice of her own. She speaks for God." As a prophet, her call was to challenge people to live abundantly. To live the life for which God had created them. She refused to accept the way they were living, so she did what it took to change things. The government was making all sorts of promises to give land to the settlers, and Dorothy called them on it. And she never budged. "She went ahead and did what she thought was right, and never let them wear her down."

Brother Jeronimo met her in 1982. "Wherever the poor needed help she'd be there. When it was raining hard or she couldn't get through she'd leave her scooter in the nearest house and head off on foot. She'd make a point of sleeping in wayside chapels—simple shelters with grass roofs. She counseled the farmers, lived with them, and ate what little they had to offer."

Like them, she suffered from malaria and the diseases of poverty: stomach cramps, worms, and tropical sores. One of her friends told me how the settlers had been dumped on the Trans-Amazonian Highway, "like a herd of cattle. We were left to get on with it. There was no school, no nothing. The government wasn't interested in the little people."

Dorothy knew that God's heart is with the little people. "We can't talk about the poor," she once wrote. "We must be poor with the poor and then there is no doubt how to act." She walked the walk. And because she challenged the status quo, challenged the government to come good on its promises, and challenged the large landowners to be satisfied with what they had instead of cornering everything for themselves, she found herself making enemies at all levels.

In 2004 her name appeared in the annual report of the Pastoral Lands Commission on the list of those marked to die. She was the second highest target in the country. The price on her head was $25,000.

And so we return to where I started this essay. That rainy day in 2005. The trail winding through the dense forest. A woman's body huddled on the ground. Baggy Bermuda shorts, stained T-shirt, baseball cap. A cloth bag containing hand-drawn maps and a battered Bible lie next to her body while a gentle rain falls, mingling her blood with the red clay of the forest floor.

In Dorothy, I found a model of the woman I strive to be. She was an activist, practical, not afraid to get her hands dirty and her feet muddy as she trekked through the forest. An idealist who challenged people to observe the high standards she observed herself, she always looked for that little spark of good she was convinced was to be found in everyone.

She was fun and funny. She loved to dance, to watch football with a beer in her hand. She loved ice cream. And peanut butter. And pancakes. A born educator, she encouraged and empowered her people to take responsibility for their lives. A leader, she understood the need for women and men to create a new relationship with the earth, valuing one another equally, welcoming diversity, and caring for the land.

A radical feminist, who knows if Dorothy, in her secret heart, would have been a candidate for ordination if the way had been open to her? Since it wasn't, she quietly went about God's work, always smiling, never openly defying the hierarchy, and making sure she was true to the principles of her religious community, as a woman with a heart as wide as the world, choosing to work for the poorest of the poor in the most abandoned places.

It was a choice that was to cost her life. But as Dorothy stood there alone, facing her killers and calmly reading from the Beatitudes, she must have known that she had been true to her vows. And I am sure that, at that moment, the trumpets were sounding on the other side as Dorothy stepped through into glory.

Twenty centuries after the death and resurrection of Christ, how shall we live our one life confidently and courageously, in such a way that it makes a difference? In a time of deep division within the Church, when fundamental differences seem to endanger its very survival, how can we, as people of faith, remain true to our calling to be the light of the world?

How do we reconcile on the one hand the concerns of the institutional Church that seeks to preserve traditional doctrines and purge dissent, with the desire of those who feel that the time has come to radically reevaluate what it means to follow Jesus? How much longer will the Church deny the potential of the women who quietly get on with the business of being Church while those in charge seek to cling to power and assert their control?

God's work is being done by people like Dorothy, and many others who choose the consecrated life at a time when so many things are militating against it. Radical feminists in the tradition of St. Hildegard of Bingen, St. Teresa of Avila, St. Catherine of Siena, and St. Thérèse of Lisieux. Women who challenge the tired, old status quo and force us to look deep inside our hearts to remember: God calls us to be transformed.

....

Binka Le Breton runs the Iracambi Rainforest Research Center (Iracambi, Brazil), and lectures and broadcasts internationally on rain forest and human rights topics. She is also president of Amigos de Iracambi, one of a number of small nonprofits working to conserve the resources of the rain forest while improving the economic situation of the local people. Le Breton is the author of The Greatest Gift: the Courageous Life and Martyrdom of Sister Dorothy Stang, *as well as* Voices from the Amazon *and* Where the Road Ends: A Home in the Brazilian Rainforest.

Those Preachin' Women

MAURICE J. NUTT, C.Ss.R., D.MIN.

"A woman in harmony with her spirit is like a river flowing.
She goes where she will without pretense and arrives at her
destination prepared to be herself and only herself."

—Maya Angelou

"I think women have always had influence within our own
communities and always will. So if I can't preach in the church,
that's all right with me. I can preach in the school. I can preach
in the home. I can preach on the bus. I can preach on the train.
I can preach on the street."

—Sister Thea Bowman

"Intense love does not measure; it just gives."

—Blessed Mother Teresa of Calcutta

I am not one of those people who seemingly has an addiction to reading
the daily obituaries in the local newspaper. However, on one particular
morning—August 15, 2012, to be exact—I came across an intriguing
obituary of a Catholic Sister in the *Chicago Sun-Times*. I did not know
this Sister, and yet I stopped to read her obituary not because I am a
Catholic priest and religious myself, but because the retelling of this
Sister's eighty-five years of life and ministry occupied a quarter of a page
of a secular newspaper.

This Franciscan Sister of the Sacred Heart, June Does, had spent most
of her religious life in hospital ministry as an X-ray technician, and after
her "retirement," she continued to work in the development department
to raise needed funds for the hospital. Sister Does had celebrated her
eighty-fifth birthday the previous year and, in giving her remarks at her

birthday party, she made a simple, yet profound statement that I found captivating. She said, "If you have a positive attitude and are willing to give of yourself, you will have a good life."

This woman religious, whom I did not know and who evidently touched many lives through her valiant ministry, had touched my life that morning with a simple statement that is, I believe, at the heart of religious life. The phrases, "positive attitude," "willing to give of yourself," and "have a good life" resonate with me. While not a particularly new notion, these words remind me of the lives, ministries, and dedication of three positive, giving, and life-loving religious women who formed, nurtured, and greatly influenced my vocation and ministry.

I am a preacher today because of the surnames Cannon, Bowman, and Delaplane, more properly acknowledged as Sister Kathleen Cannon, OP; Sister Thea Bowman, FSPA; and Sister Joan Delaplane, OP. I like to call these Sisters, "those preachin' women."

I cannot say that when I began my journey to the priesthood I sought out women to be my homiletic professors. All I wanted to be was an effective preacher of God's word. I had long witnessed the notoriously uninspiring homilies given by some priests, and I knew that something had to be different; something had to change.

It was my desire that my preaching be biblically based, theologically sound, and culturally aware, while also being stimulating, motivating, and relevant. I also knew in large part that "the words of my mouth and the meditations of my heart" must be acceptable to God and, therefore, not be about me.

To my surprise and my delight, those assigned to instruct me in preaching, as both a seminarian and a priest, were all women. I had wanted something different and that's exactly what I got. For some it might seem strange having women prepare priests to preach the Gospel.

Only men—priests and deacons—are the official preachers within the context of Eucharistic liturgies. In essence, these women who were well-trained and qualified to teach homiletics could not officially practice what they taught men to do. While it is not my purpose here to argue this canonical law of our Church, I am most grateful for those "preachin' women" who instilled in me a love for the proclamation of God's word.

I also am most grateful for those biblical women who bore witness to God's word. It was our Blessed Mother, Mary, who was overshadowed by the Holy Spirit and became the mother of the Savior of the world, Jesus, the "Word made flesh and dwelt among us." Mary cried out, "My soul proclaims the greatness of the Lord, my spirit rejoices in God my savior."

It was Mary who encouraged the first miracle of Jesus. It was Mary who lingered, lovingly, at the cross, Mary, who was present on the day of Pentecost and received the fullness of the Holy Spirit and witnessed to its power. And it was another Mary, Mary of Magdala, who not only was compelled by the persuasion of Jesus's compassion and preaching, but who also first witnessed the resurrection and did not hesitate to announce, "He lives!"

Yes, those biblical feminine forebearers waited on the Word, bore the Word, received the Word, nurtured the Word, loved the Word, and announced the Word; yes, those preachin' women!

Sister Kathleen Cannon, OP

I met Dominican Sister of Peace Kathleen Cannon as I began my studies at Catholic Theological Union in Chicago, in 1985. I wanted to be a preacher, so I concentrated my studies in the areas of word and worship that allowed me to specialize in liturgy. It also provided an opportunity to be mentored in preaching by Sister Kathleen.

She was a meticulous teacher who demanded arduous homily preparation and homily development. As testament to her many helpful directives, I still have the written homily critiques that she gave me. They serve the purpose of keeping me grounded in the firm foundation that I received as a budding preacher. The written critiques also remind me of the dedication Sister Kathleen had for me to learn the techniques of preaching, as well as a deep reverence for the word of God.

Unknowingly, I believe that it was Sister Kathleen's personal passion and commitment to training future preachers that sowed the seed in me to one day become a preaching professor. I remember watching Sister Kathleen in class one day and thinking, "I would like to help form preachers, too." I humbly pray that I may be half the teacher that Sister Kathleen was for me.

At this writing, Sister Kathleen Cannon, OP, is the associate dean of the College of Science at the University of Notre Dame and concurrent associate professor of theology. She is also a specialist in homiletics [preaching preparation and delivery—ed.] and is a frequent contributor to pastoral and homiletic publications.

Sister Thea Bowman, FSPA

No one really "met" Franciscan Sister of Perpetual Adoration Thea Bowman; no, you encountered her! Her bold, inviting, and dramatic personality drew you to her. Sister Thea passed over twenty years ago and yet her spirit remains with me, so much so that it is difficult for me to write about her in the past tense.

I "encountered" Sister Thea in 1984: a year that brought many challenges in her life. That year, Sister Thea's parents both died and she was diagnosed with breast cancer. I met her at the annual gathering of African American Catholic bishops, priests, deacons (and their wives), religious men and women, and seminarians held at Xavier University in

New Orleans. I was a young seminarian and this was my first opportunity to meet our African American Catholic leadership.

I remember Sister Thea giving a moving talk on what it means to be black and Catholic. Until that time I had been isolated as the only African American in my seminary formation program, and I never realized how much I missed my cultural expressions. As Sister Thea spoke her words touched my very being; when she began to sing, I started to cry uncontrollably. It was a cathartic moment for me. I no longer felt alone in my journey to the priesthood. I had come home and would not have to take on or assimilate into someone else's culture because I had my own rich African American culture and other religious men and women to support me.

The very next summer, I enrolled in the Institute for Black Catholic Studies at Xavier University, where Sister Thea, in 1980, had been a founding faculty member. It would be a few years later that Sister Thea would actually be my teacher, but her presence was felt there nevertheless.

While Sister Thea held an earned doctorate in English literature, had been published, and was in demand nationally and internationally as a speaker and preacher, being with her at Xavier was like having your mother in school with you. Although a consummate educator, competent and articulate, Sister Thea preferred to operate in her notable Mississippi folksy manner.

She would walk around campus being bold and boisterous. Her personality was so overwhelming that it took a moment to decipher if she were really real. She would tell the black students to go break up the group of white students sitting together in the cafeteria. Sister Thea wanted them to have to get out of their comfort zones, to dialogue and get to know black folks. She believed that teaching transcended the classroom. For Sister Thea, the world was the classroom and every moment was a teachable moment.

As an educator, Sister Thea's pedagogy was to motivate her students to be self-determined and inquisitive learners. On more than one occasion while teaching, she would abruptly stop the class lecture to make sure that her students were not merely memorizing the subject material, but fully comprehending and internalizing the lesson. She would often quip, "So what this [subject matter] have to do with your life, your family, your community, your ministry, or your lived experience?" Be assured that Sister Thea's questions were never rhetorical; they demanded a response. She had no problem telling a classroom of fully functioning adults to stand up and speak up!

Humorously she would challenge her students by asking the ambiguous, yet loaded, question: "Who's teaching this class?" If her students responded, "You're teaching this class," she would then ask, "Are you sure? Am I teaching this class or are you teachers as well?" The point she was impressing upon her students was that in the educational process— through dialogue, examination, and exploration—we learn from one another. She wanted her disciples to be confident that in the learning environment that they were both learners and teachers. "Each one, teach one" was her constant mantra.

Sister Thea would often ask her students to self-evaluate; to give themselves a grade. Then she would look intently at the grades the students had given themselves, and ask the students why they had given themselves that particular grade. If the students either overrated or underrated themselves, Sister Thea would gently tell the students to "think long and hard" and reevaluate themselves. There were times when students would continue to underrate themselves and she would let the grade stand! This experimentation was a lesson in itself for her students, to be both truthful and confident in their abilities.

I can honestly say that Sister Thea didn't teach me how to preach.

Rather, she helped me find my authentic voice as a preacher. While her exuberant preaching inspired her students, I believe that it was her authenticity that attracted others to listen, learn, and be stirred into action. At all times, Sister Thea was truly herself. She was comfortable and confident in her own skin.

Many people felt that Sister Thea was someone who spoke off the cuff. Being in her presence, it seemed that anything that came up, came out. Yes, she was unquestionably spontaneous, yet I believe that most of the words she spoke in sermon or song were deliberate and well-calculated. She was most intentional in all that she said and did. That's the gift she gave me as a friend, spiritual mother, teacher, and mentor. She wanted me always to live authentically and intentionally with integrity.

Sister Thea would often say to the students she taught in her preaching courses, "How am I supposed to believe what you are saying, if you don't believe it yourself? Preach with confidence and conviction, or sit down!" That lesson has remained with me. I now preach what I believe and believe what I preach.

Due to her illness, Sister Thea was unable to attend my ordination to the priesthood in June of 1989. The following month, I joined a large group of her friends, colleagues, and students from the Institute for Black Catholic Studies who made a pilgrimage to Canton, Mississippi, to pay tribute to Sister Thea before she was called to be with the Lord.

That July afternoon we met in the parish of her youth, Holy Child Jesus, and gave back to her all that she had poured into us in through her teaching and preaching. The afternoon was filled with song, praise, preaching, poetry, drama, and dance. Sister Thea said, "Thank you for giving me my flowers while I am still here!"

Because the cancer had ravaged her body and had now entered her bones, we were cautioned not to touch Sister Thea because it was too painful for her. I went to her and kneeled before her in her wheelchair and asked for her blessing on my life and my priesthood. As painful as it was for her, she stretched her feeble hands out and laid them on my head in blessing.

In a real sense, I felt that my priestly ordination culminated with her imposition of hands. Little did I know then, but Sister Thea was passing the torch. Now I teach the preaching classes she taught at the Institute for Black Catholic Studies. She remains with me in the pulpit and in my preaching. Before I preach, I always pray to Sister Thea, asking for her intercession. I feel her presence ever with me.

Sister Thea knew no stranger. She offered compassion to the young man living with AIDS. She enjoyed a hearty laugh with her beloved "old folks," the elders of her community. She met and enchanted celebrities such as Harry Belafonte and Whoopi Goldberg. She encouraged single mothers. She spoke strong words couched in love to the Roman Catholic hierarchy. Yet her greatest testimony may have been the way she faced death, living life fully until the end. That inspirational courage, that outlook, spoke to all cultures.

During her fifty-two years on earth, Sister Thea Bowman wove the diverse elements of her life into a garment as vivid and vibrant as her African garb. She was simultaneously an "old folks child" steeped in the traditions of her people, a devoted Franciscan, an advocate of all cultures while maintaining her love for her "own black self," a proud maiden of Mississippi, a persuasive preacher, a tenacious teacher, a soul-stirring singer, a lover of the Church, a teller of the "true truth," a faithful friend, a spiritual mother to many, and an instrument of peace, love, and joy.

Before she died, she declared, "I want people to remember that I tried to love the Lord…that I tried to love them, and how that computes is immaterial." She tried to weave that garment until the very end—little bit by little bit.

Sister Joan Delaplane, OP

"If every frightened, paralyzed follower of Christ, hiding in their upper rooms, were to open themselves to the gift and grace of hope, given by the Spirit, might we not see a transformation of this country's values before it is too late? Might not the anger and courage proceeding from this hope make a difference right here? The action might be as simple as a phone call or letter to our legislators, or getting out to the polls to vote. We need to remember, of course, that as long as we Christians just talk about a kingdom of peace and justice, the world will tolerate us. Action to bring it about and to undo oppressive structures will be another thing. Just ask Jeremiah; just ask Jesus; just ask Martin Luther King, Jr., or Oscar Romero!"

These words by Sister Joan Delaplane, a Dominican Sister from Adrian, Michigan, taken from a 2002 reflection she gave titled, "And the Greatest of These Is Hope," based on 1 Peter 3:15, is one of the reasons I wanted to meet and be mentored by her. Literally, her words proceeded from her. I had heard that this Sister could *preach*!

I later learned that Sister Joan had taught elementary and high school for twenty-five years in various parts of Michigan. Having been in religious life for over sixty years, at this writing she is professor emerita at the Aquinas Institute of Theology in St. Louis, Missouri, where she taught homiletics from 1977 to 2002. She was the first woman and first Catholic to be President of the Academy of Homiletics.

Sister Joan has had broad experience in preaching, directing retreats, and conducting workshops in preaching for both Catholic and Protestant ministers. Spiritual direction has been her avocation the past twenty-five years, and is now her principal ministry.

I vividly remember sitting in Sister Joan's office as a newly accepted doctoral student in the then-recently established doctor of ministry program in preaching at Aquinas Institute of Theology, which she directed. It remains the only Catholic doctoral program in preaching in the country. She had heard of me as well, and was affirming of my preaching abilities. Yet she warned me that the doctoral preaching program was rigorous and demanding, and that even though I was a busy pastor, I had to make the time and commitment to the program.

That initial meeting germinated into a deep respect for her knowledge, competency, and spirit. Sister Joan sought the very best from her students; she definitely did not allow us to sit on our potential. Her critique of my preaching was always spot-on. She would not permit our preaching events to become predictable. Finding our "preaching default" was second nature to her. She would lead us toward using variety in our preaching by introducing different and sometimes challenging homiletic options.

Sister Joan has always been cognizant of the Holy Spirit working in her life, and I believe that the Holy Spirit is her primary source of guidance and strength. In *The Living Word: An Overshadowing of the Spirit,* she wrote that "without consciousness of the place of God's Spirit, the whole preaching endeavor for some individuals may easily become overwhelming and discouraging; for others, simply an ego trip." I ultimately learned from Sister Joan that preaching was indisputedly the work of the Holy Spirit. One had to be open to the prompting and influence of the Holy Spirit in order to be an effective preacher.

Sister Joan encouraged me and nurtured me to be a Spirit-filled black preacher within the context of the Roman Catholic Church. She, this white woman from Michigan, would remind me that within the context of black preaching, the preacher is expected to be anointed by the power of the Holy Spirit before there is any attempt to preach the word. She said it, and I believed it, that regardless of one's ability, strength, or style, the sermon or homily is ultimately a product of the power of the Holy Spirit, which enables the preacher to utter, "Thus says the Lord." It is the sacred memory of Sister Joan's teaching and preaching that has helped me evolve into the preacher I am today. Thank you, God, and thank you, Sister Joan!

It is somewhat baffling for me to imagine that these three "women of the word" would dedicate much of their lives and ministries to the formation of men to preach the Gospel—a ministry that officially at Mass they are not allowed to perform. What would make them do for others what they could not do themselves?

The cure to my incredulous pondering is that, much like Sister June Does, whose obituary caught my eye, Sister Kathleen, Sister Thea, and Sister Joan had positive attitudes and wanted to give of themselves, and thus live good lives. I believe that their deep love for the Church and for God's word compelled them to unselfishly form future priests to preach the Gospel so that generations would come to know, love and serve God.

To those "preachin' women" and to all religious women who have formed and nurtured my faith, I simply say "thank you." Because of you, I am a preacher.

....

Maurice J. Nutt, C.Ss.R., D.Min., is an internationally noted revival, mission, and retreat preacher. Father Nutt is also a faculty member at the Institute for Black Catholic Studies at Xavier University in New Orleans, Louisiana, where he teaches preaching. He is a member of the Chicago-based Redemptorist Parish Mission Team.

Witness for Peace: Joan Chittister

TERESA WILSON

Many people know Joan Chittister, a Benedictine Sister of Erie, as a bestselling author and international lecturer on topics of justice, peace, human rights, women's issues, and contemporary spirituality in the Church and in society. Joan, as a peace activist, began to influence my thinking when I met her in 1984.

She had responded to an invitation from Peace Links, a then-new initiative founded by U.S. congressional wives to educate women on the threat of nuclear war. Joan came to speak at an early funding event in Pittsburgh and returned several times, always bringing out the biggest crowds we ever attracted. She was a prophetic voice, giving a historical view of the condition of women in religion and in society as a challenge to the peace movement. Her analysis of violence against women—physical, social, and psychological—gave women in the peace movement the words to stand up against militarism and sexism. "Sister Joan says what I think but don't have words or courage to say," was an oft-repeated comment.

Joan had had a radio audience for years, from repeated appearances on the Chicago Sunday Evening Club's interfaith program, *30 Good Minutes*. And she had been speaking in Erie, Pennsylvania, where her Benedictine order is an important presence for women.

She spoke "truth to power" in a way that encouraged our movement and gave us strength for the hard anti–nuclear war advocacy role that we had taken on. Betty Bumpers, wife of Senator Dale Bumpers of Arkansas, was organizing women all over the country to respond to the reality that it was women who were home to answer their children's questions about the very present fear of nuclear war, while at the same time their husbands in the U.S. Senate were making decisions in response to the nuclear threat. Peace Links, which I helped to lead, was a women's movement response to the nuclear threat.

My first meetings with Joan led to shared interests in women's concerns and efforts that spanned the past twenty-five years. She joined my effort with the Grail, a decades-old international laywomen's organization that has blossomed over the years into interfaith membership. Many years ago the Grail had invited sixteen-year-old Joan; but so, too, had the Benedictines.

Today Grail women, scattered in various parts of the world, follow Joan in books, videos, and public-speaking appearances. We support her worldwide as she feeds our understanding of women in the Church and in society.

Closer to my home, in Pittsburgh, in workshops at Carlow University and also at the Thomas Merton Center's annual dinner, where she was awarded the New People Award, Joan gave us the words and the courage to speak out for peace and for justice.

She has given voice to many women and yes, to men as well, as we increasingly view the world through her feminist perspective. It's one that challenges, as she says, "religious life that is spiritually patriarchal in origin, a society hierarchical in structure, and a world so single-sexed in vision that it sees with only one eye, hears with only one ear and thinks with one half of the human brain," as Joan says, "and it shows."

Joan is fond of saying that in 1994 I made her join a group of Pittsburgh women who were planning to be a part of the Peace Train from Helsinki, Finland, to Beijing, China. Joan joined us for the seven-thousand-mile, monthlong train trip through nine countries to Beijing, where the United Nations' Fourth World Conference on Women would open in September 1995. The initiative was sponsored by the Women's International League for Peace and Freedom (WILPF).

She had decided that the monthlong trip with three hundred female peace activists could be good preparation for a teaching assignment in Cambridge, England, where she was a St. Edmund Fellow. The *National Catholic Reporter*, where she published a weekly column, would cover the story and print her commentary from along the way.

The Peace Train took us from Helsinki through the cities of St. Petersburg, Russia; Kiev, Ukraine; Sofia, Bulgaria; and Bucharest, Romania; continuing to Istanbul, Turkey; and through central Asia with a stop in Alma Ata, Kazakhstan; then days of awesome isolation in western China before the train eventually arrived in Beijing.

Joan participated in meetings with women at each of the stops on the twenty-five-day odyssey to take their stories to Beijing. There a plan for action would be created to advocate a focus on women at the U.N. Joan reported back to the *National Catholic Reporter* from the Peace Train and then, in Beijing, from both the official government and nongovernment conferences.

Between times, Joan found space and quiet in spite of the bedlam created by peace activists aged twenty to eighty-four. She could be seen often in one of the coach cars, swapping tales and trading stories among some of the Peace Train passengers who had become her new friends. In the Benedictine spirit, she knew how to have a good time.

At the same time Joan's perspective and analysis, which was widely read, was a valuable gift of her talents to thousands of women. She shared the heartfelt stories she had gathered, and gave life to their desperate situations. Later, with her Benedictine colleagues at Benetvision (her monastery-based publishing ministry), she published a video and a book on the Peace Train adventure and on the Fourth World Conference on Women.

The original intention of WILPF was to take the stories of women from the newly independent countries to Beijing, but Joan did more. She shared their stories with many people in her international audience beyond the conference, who heard about these women for the first time. Being with Joan on the train was an opportunity to enjoy her lively wit, her ability to make the most of the moment. I came to appreciate how hard she worked to get into print the poignant stories we were hearing from women who had no other opportunity to take these stories to the conference. Joan heard their need to make life more than survival in these post-Soviet countries, where, after the state-mandated inclusion of women ended in the workforce, on the battlefield, and in education, women had been sent back into their homes.

The violence against women and the need for halfway houses to escape angry and defeated men was a repeated theme. Joan quoted Evelyn Burke, "there is a time when forbearance is no longer a virtue." I think of that quote now as Joan faces the crisis of the leadership of women religious being rebuked by Vatican officials.

At each stop of the Peace Train—remember, this was in the mid-1990s—we scrambled to find access to the technology to get her *NCR* articles back to the United States. It was a challenge. The famous steps in Odessa (seen in the classic movie *The Battleship Potemkin*) were a memorable part of the search for a sending site in Odessa, Turkey. Ultimately, she did meet her deadlines!

Another memory: In Eastern Russia we had to stop to change the wheels on our train, to accommodate a shift to narrow-gauge track in this remote area. We stood in a field watching men working with rudimentary equipment and no safety gear, lifting the rail cars and changing the wheels. Women from the area arrived at the scene with tubs of steaming corn on the cob. Joan was among the most appreciative—far from Pennsylvania, even unbuttered field corn tasted good! But it was the strength, the resourcefulness, and friendliness of the women that impressed us, and Joan reveled in it.

Joan's press pass at the conferences in Beijing gave her the opportunity to share the government and NGO agendas, including all the demands in the plan for action, which was accepted at Beijing. Of all the resolutions debated and passed, Joan thought that gender sensitivity was the new demand on every government that could not be dodged when they returned home. She quoted my favorite voice from Beijing, Gertrude Mongella, Tanzanian chair of the NGO conference. Gertrude pleaded men to join women in the challenge and struggle for gender equality, just as women had joined men in the struggles against colonialism and apartheid.

Joan said, "In Beijing my whole life was confirmed. Women who speak for women are often verbally attacked, but I will speak for women to the edge of my grave—the Girl Child [girls of the world] depends on me." She defined her feminism as "Christianity given respect."

Joan came home, as many of us did, to share our rich experiences with any women's groups we could get in front of. None did it as well or as often as did Joan. On one occasion she addressed the American Association of University Women (AAUW). She told that group that she considered the most important events in history to be, one, the Ice Age; two, the Industrial Revolution; and three, the women's movement. So, when the question of why a Fourth World Conference on Women was held, she answered, "It's recognition of women as one half the population whose human rights were not given, but which could not be taken away."

Trademarks of Joan's long public career are her wit and storytelling gifts. I remember an early "speaking truth to power" incident that continues to amuse me. It is a story that takes place within a gathering of men held in foreign territory for her—a fancy reception for business executives in Texas. Their complaints about the effect of Mexico on Texas and their fortunes, and what was to be done, elicited a conversation-stopping response from Joan, "Well, we could give it back to them!"

Joan's books have been a continuing source of new thinking and honest questioning. *In Search of Belief* and *Called to Question: A Spiritual Memoir* shared courageous insight and awareness and a growing capacity to reinterpret the familiar texts. They are two of the books that show Joan's gifts to many of us, with examples of her ability to use questions to raise consciousness and increase critical thinking and understanding.

A not-often-quoted book, *The Way We Were: A Story of Conversion and Renewal*, describes the transformation of her beloved Benedictines from pre– to post–Vatican II nuns. It serves as a heartfelt review of just how difficult and challenging change is for women in religious communities.

I remember Joan in 2004 during her encounter with the Vatican over her participation in a meeting in Ireland where the ordination of women in the Catholic Church would be discussed. Many of us know the moving story of how the Erie Benedictines stood behind Joan in her insistence that her right to be a part of that discussion was clearly within the Benedictine Order definition of faithful obedience. That's not the demanded unquestioning obedience, but an ancient Benedictine definition of obedience based on listening.

There were tense weeks as Vatican officials called the prioress of her Erie community to Rome to review Joan's position and to demand that she forbid Joan from speaking at the Dublin conference. Yet her Sisters' unwavering support brought the incident to closure. Since that time of open challenge to the Vatican, Joan has been unwelcome in many dioceses, where she previously had received many invitations to speak and share her writing.

In the millennium year of 2000, U.N. Secretary-General Kofi Annan announced the Global Peace Initiative of Women (GPIW). Joan became cochair and, since then, has been instrumental in creating a viable organization. I attended the first meeting of this group in 2002 in Geneva, Switzerland, where Joan was one of the featured speakers at a convocation of six hundred spiritual leaders. In a crowded room where Eastern-faith adherents outnumbered Christians, hundreds of orange-robed Buddhists and white-garbed Hindus were a rapt audience for Joan.

In the context of religion-based hopes for peace and justice, Joan chose to make an explicit statement of how the issue of gender is central to global peace. She described, in detail, the discovery of the microscope and how it led to a new understanding of the importance of the science of reproduction. It is this explicit understanding—that in reproduction, women make the crucial contribution of an ovum, necessarily fertilized by the male—that is foundational for recognizing the rights of women. It was certainly not a speech that this audience expected—I held my breath—but it was wildly applauded. It remains in my memory as a breakthrough in feminist perspective, an irrefutable illustration of the value of women.

This first GPIW meeting ten years ago has been followed up by large meetings in Asia and Africa that continue to bring together women and men from all religions to promote peace. In the U.S. in recent years, GPIW called together national spiritual leaders to meet with Wall Street bankers, representatives of the Occupy Wall Street movement, environmentalists, the business community, and the academic and spiritual community in dialogue on capitalism. This was designed as a cocreative exploration of all these communities, a visionary process, taking back voices and together creating a new societal vision.

Recently Joan, a coleader in that initiative, spoke to the graduating class at Stanford University. Her message was, "Rebel, rebel, rebel. Have courage to ask the right questions, without apology, without fear and inborn close-mindedness. Refuse to tell the old lies—that there is nothing to be done about discrimination, about ending the global carnage, about providing health care and housing and food, about women raped, beaten, trafficked and silenced."

She concluded her address with a call to leadership: "Inspire in those who follow you the conviction and the will to denounce the lies, to reject the greed, to resist the heretics of inhumanity who peddle inequality, injustice, and the torturers' instruments of social violence."

As former president of the LCWR and former prioress of the Erie, Pennsylvania, Benedictine nuns, Joan is not a novice in the area of leadership. I think of earlier quotes of Joan's to audiences during the years that I have heard her speak. In one address, in 1987, echoing words from the book of Sirach, she reflected:

> Life is not even, not smooth. There is a time to heal ourselves from the hurts that weigh down and keep us from taking charge of our own emotional lives. There is a time to lose, to let go of whatever has become captive in life, old ideas, faces, and hopes. There is a time to weep tears that dignify the loss of things and people in life that have brought us to where we are today. There is a time to heal ourselves from the hurts that weigh down and keep us from taking charge of our own emotional lives. There is a time to be reborn out of old ideas, old shapes, old forms. There is a time to build up and to construct the new world, to co-create the globe so what we leave behind is better than what we received.

At this writing, in the midst of her own community's crisis, being doubted by Vatican officials, Joan was addressing an evening gathering with a talk called "Questions for a Burka." It was an attempt to understand the women of the Muslim world who are enclosed in the insulating article of clothing called a "burka." That community reflection will, no doubt, show up in her future articles and speeches. So goes the life of Joan, always pushing ahead.

....

Teresa Wilson is former leader of the Grail, a women's lay organization of about a thousand women in twenty countries, committed to social transformation. She also was a founding organizer of Pennsylvania Peace Links.

Band of Sisters

MARY FISHMAN

I had been looking forward for a long time to meeting Carol Coston, an Adrian Dominican Sister, and seeing her organic farm in Texas. When I finally got a big enough grant to pay for my film crew and me to travel there, we scheduled a shoot for April 2010. We chose a time of month when there would be no moon, so we could shoot a sky full of stars. That idea came to me after reading Carol's book *Permaculture: Finding Our Own Vines and Fig Trees*, in which she described the features of Santuario Sisterfarm, the center for cultural diversity and biodiversity she and Elise Garcia, OP, had founded in the hill country outside of San Antonio.

Reading the book, I was fascinated by Carol's description of the tower, a two-story structure with a deck on top. The idea for the tower was to get up high enough to watch the Perseid meteor showers. Built by an all-female crew, it ended up having a guest room on the ground floor and a meditation room on the second floor. The deck turned out to be a nice place for cocktails after long hot days of working on the farm. I thought a night scene with Carol and Elise on top of the tower looking at the stars would be a way to introduce audiences to the universe story, which was going to be a key part of the film.

Prior to meeting her, I was a little bit intimidated by Carol's resume: The first director of NETWORK, the national Catholic social justice lobby founded by Sisters; founder and director of two Partners for the Common Good loan funds, raising over eleven million dollars in investments from religious congregations and overseeing low-interest loans to low-income communities in the United States, Latin America, and

Africa; the only Catholic Sister ever to receive the Presidential Citizens Medal, for "exemplary deeds of service for our nation." I needn't have worried, though, because Carol is so low-key and matter-of-fact. She's such a good sport about everything, and along with Elise puts you at ease with great hospitality and great food. They live simply and richly, and they know how to have fun.

It rained often and hard the first two and a half days my crew and I were filming them, and a lot of our filming was outside. On the third and last day, as we were about to shoot several key scenes, my camera suddenly decided to conk out. We were almost an hour from downtown San Antonio, where there might or might not be a place for professional camera rentals.

While Ines Sommer, my cinematographer, tried to get the camera working, I decided to try and stay calm and be contemplative. I sat in one of two chairs in Carol and Elise's living room looking out at the beautiful view, and Carol joined me in the other chair. I remember us just sitting there, not necessarily talking about anything important. She was just there to be supportive, in her sensitive way.

Two miracles then happened, in quick succession: (1) Ines got the camera to start again by blow-drying it, getting all the dampness out, and (2) the thunderclouds cleared just in time for the stars to come out, and we got our night scene.

It had been a long road to that tower. Ten years ago I was an architect and urban planner. I was nearing the end of a ten-year stint that started out happily for me in Chicago's Department of Planning and Development but was ending up miserably in the Department of Buildings. I really wasn't feeling that my work mattered in the bigger scheme of things—frankly it was hard for me to care that much whether some large company got their permit a little bit faster because I helped them. All my professional life I had been wanting to do something to help poor people get the same advantages the rest of us had, and I kept coming up short in the jobs I got and the assignments I was given.

Disillusioned about my prospects of doing social justice work as an architect, I finally was making a move to follow my dream of being a filmmaker, a dream that had been awakened in high school, at Mother McAuley, an all-girls school run by the Sisters of Mercy in Chicago. Mother McAuley in the early to mid-1970s was full of experimentation and idealism and joy, at least for me. There weren't that many Sisters around who were teaching at that point, but they were still in administration and their influence permeated the school.

And I did have three or four teachers who were Sisters, professional women who were tops in their field and held themselves and their students to the highest standards. Nothing was worse than being given a sharp look by Sister Simeon when I squeaked out a wrong note on my viola. But it was worth it to be in her orchestra class every morning, waking up to great songs like "The Infernal Galop" from *Orpheus in the Underworld* (the can-can) or "June Is Bustin' Out All Over" from *Carousel*, and to the sight of Sister conducting and dancing to the music. Playing in Sister Simeon's orchestra for four years, I felt how powerful and moving it could be to create something with other people.

Mother McAuley really stressed media studies, and sent its graduates to college knowing how to think critically and how to write. In English class my senior year we studied film. We watched movies on TV at home, wrote about them, analyzed them, studied camera moves, and drew storyboards for our own short stories, and I loved it. I made a small effort to find a college that had a film school, but ended up at the University of Notre Dame, which didn't. Instead it offered a great architecture program (which fit my love of drawing and history) and set me off into studies and a profession that I enjoyed for many years.

But back to ten years ago. I had already finished a few film classes at night, was working in the building department by day, when Rita, my eighty-seven-year-old mother and best friend, became very sick, had surgery, and needed a lot of help from then on, so much so that I eventually quit my job to take care of her—to be her "curator," as she dubbed it. This freed me to say I was going to make a film in my spare time. And I already knew the topic: the three-hundred-year history of nuns in the United States.

Now where did that come from? My sister Patty had given me a book one day by David Snowdon, Ph.D., called, *Aging with Grace: What the Nun Study Teaches Us About Leading Longer, Healthier, and More Meaningful Lives*, about Sisters in an Alzheimer's study. In handing the book over, Patty said, "you should do a movie about this." Perfect! Since I was certainly looking for a more meaningful life, why not make a film about women who already had one?

As I read *Aging with Grace*, I was surprised at how alive these women were, many of whom were in their eighties and nineties. Though I had had Sisters as teachers in high school and elementary school, I never thought of them as real people. I never had one as a friend, never thought of them as having come from families like mine, as having hopes and dreams and disappointments and frailties. They just seemed above the human condition somehow, until I read this book.

So I started reading all I could about the history of women religious in this country. Volumes and volumes about the arrival of small groups of women from Europe, who in short order and with very little money founded schools and hospitals and orphanages. I read about what life was like for Sisters in the 1700s and 1800s when they were intrepid pioneers, how things became more regimented and controlled by Rome in the early 1900s, and how Vatican II opened things up in the 1960s and beyond.

I was surprised to learn of Sisters' involvement in the civil rights, feminist, peace, gay and lesbian, and environmental movements, and of their efforts for justice for women in the Church. And not so surprised that more than a few men in the Catholic Church hierarchy (and some lay Catholics) didn't appreciate the changes most Sisters had made since Vatican II.

The more I read, the more I was amazed at what Sisters in this country had accomplished. It's impossible to imagine the United States without the marvelous institutions and organizations they founded and the spiritual influence they have had. And I also became very angry—at the stereotypes, the ridicule, and the trivialization of Sisters in popular culture. I thought that a film presenting the Sisters as they really are and for what they did might help change their image, and give them the credit they deserve.

People told me that my topic—three centuries of Sisters' work—was too broad, and I had to agree. It was in writing a grant application for investors looking to fund a social-activist bent that I decided to focus my film on Catholic Sisters in the United States and their work for social justice after Vatican II. Thank God for that grant (which I ended up not even applying for), because once I settled on a social justice theme, where my interest really lay, the road opened up.

I thought I was going to make a film about action—where Sisters working on one great cause after another would show us how it's done and inspire us to do it ourselves, how to skillfully overcome the opposition and put the bad guys in their place. The one thing I didn't understand was how deeply contemplation, prayer, and the practice of nonviolence are behind all this action. I got more than an inkling of this from my first conference call, in June 2006, with a focus group of Sisters (Nancy Sylvester, IHM; Margaret Galiardi, OP; Carol Coston, OP; and

Mary Daniel Turner, SNDdeN) that Nancy had gathered to help me set the scope and direction of the film.

On this call, and in subsequent conversations, new words, new concepts, and new people were presented to me. It was a lot to take in. I learned that it was a profound contemplative experience that led Sisters to be concerned with the things of this world. And that this concern was evolving into a concept of justice not just for people, but for the earth and all beings.

It was from this group that I first heard about Pat Siemen, OP, and her remarkable Center for Earth Jurisprudence, which promotes the rights of the natural world, and about Miriam MacGillis, OP, a mentor to so many Sisters and to people the world over from her base at Genesis Farm in Blairstown, New Jersey.

And I was introduced to the new cosmology, to which many Sisters were being drawn. Also called the "universe story," the new cosmology integrates new understandings about the nature of the universe, the interconnectedness of life, and our role as humans on the planet with a quest for the Divine.

I spent the next six years absorbing as much as I could through conversation, reading, and my own contemplation about how to work this spirituality into the film and into my life. God was changing for me in so many ways, and I was changing in the process.

Around the same time I started talking to Sisters about the film, I signed up for spiritual direction with a Sister. I needed help in taking care of Rita. My reasoning in seeking out a Sister for spiritual direction was that, unlike a therapist, who would tell me to put my mother in a nursing home and take care of myself first, a Catholic Sister would encourage my self-sacrifice and just help me get through it.

I was wrong about that. When Rita's health became much worse, and caring for her brought me to the limits of my capacity, my spiritual director, Mary Ruth Broz, RSM, would quote Deuteronomy 30:19, "I have set before you life and death, blessings and curses. Choose life so that you and your descendants may live." "Choose life," she would say to me. She opened the door for me to the possibility that we might not be able to keep Rita at home, that I might be forgiven if I said I just can't do it anymore. It helped me to have that out.

Rita died peacefully at home half a year later. I had been helping her full-time for six years, and it took me a long time to grieve and recuperate. Mary Ruth accompanied me through Rita's death. Our sessions since then have helped bring me to new life. She listens without judgment, guides me to find the sacred in my experiences, and champions me like a mother.

Lillian Murphy, RSM, says about Sisters, "we are the risk-takers of the church. We are down there with the people, we know what the needs are." She could be talking about Mary Ruth, or about Pat Murphy and JoAnn Persch, both Sisters of Mercy, two of the main characters in my film. Pat and JoAnn have spent a lot of time in the past forty years with people who are broken down (survivors of torture, battered women, prisoners), which is not easy to do, day-in and day-out. Patiently and compassionately, they give people the space to draw from their own well of strength and dignity.

With an intimate knowledge of what people need, they work for justice, to change the structures that oppress people. When they saw immigrant detainees being denied their basic human right to have pastoral care in prison, they were instrumental in getting a law passed in Illinois that guarantees this right. They dogged the jail officials when they dragged their feet implementing the new law, organized an interfaith team of volunteers to provide the pastoral care, and continue to go themselves with the team every week.

Following Pat and JoAnn's story over four years, I have been to the School of the Americas Watch in Columbus, Georgia, and to rallies, prayer services, and conferences for immigrants. I've had a taste of what it's like to deal with I.C.E. (Immigrations and Customs Enforcement), and what it's like to lobby politicians. I've also lived a lot of the last sixty-some years vicariously because, between them as Sisters, they've been everywhere and done everything, and they're good at telling stories about it. They're my neighbors, and I hope that we'll have a long time to enjoy each other now that the movie is finished.

I can't imagine how the film would have turned out without Nancy Sylvester's involvement. Her own life experience and her analysis of what Sisters have been about in the past fifty years and what's happening now is so integral to the telling of the story.

Nancy was the second national coordinator of NETWORK and is a past-president of the LCWR. Her current work is on the transforma- tion of consciousness. Feeling that we are at an impasse in our political systems, our religious institutions, and our relationship with the planet, she founded the Institute for Communal Contemplation and Dialogue. Her institute offers a variety of retreats where people can begin to explore and engage this impasse together in contemplation.

I took part in one of Nancy's one-day retreats, and am now part of a follow-up group she and Margaret Galiardi lead, which meets via conference calls. The concept of these groups is not to try and solve the world's problems, but rather to change our own consciousness so that we might see and approach these problems differently. All I can say, as a beginner, is that it is a luxury to sit with people in contemplative silence, and to practice listening to each other with a compassionate heart.

One of the things that developed through spiritual direction, my friendship with Pat and JoAnn, and my involvement with the movie, is that I recently became an Associate of the Sisters of Mercy. As an Associate you feel like you are part of a loving community, and part of a tradition that goes way back. This is tradition in the best sense of the word—wisdom and customs passed down from generations that tie people together in a common sense of purpose and values.

I appreciate the professionalism of Sisters, the hospitality, the sense that we're all in this together and we're here to help each other, the way people in a village must have felt. Sisters *are* the risk-takers of the Church—they stand up for women, refugees, gays and lesbians, and prisoners, no matter the cost. They have an openness to what the future holds and to where the Spirit is leading. This is what inspires me and attracts me to Sisters of all congregations.

And I feel like I've found a spiritual home. It is the Sisters who are asking the deeper questions that the teaching arm of the Catholic Church hasn't yet been considering. What does it tell us about ourselves to know that everything in our universe came from the same source 13.7 billion years ago? What can it tell us about God? How precious is this Earth with all these interdependent beings, and how should we behave as part of it? These are urgent questions, because if we don't begin to understand our role as humans differently, we will eventually be the cause of a massive extinction of life on Earth. Catholic Sisters are creating safe spaces in which to ask these questions and to explore the answers.

Ten years ago, before my reconnection with Sisters, I had a vague idea about wanting to live in the country, to be closer to nature and to God. After all I've seen and experienced since then, I'm now thinking about a small organic farm on a prairie, with some kind of community involvement. I want to see the stars at night. Maybe I'll build a tower. I'll still make movies, too. And I have the feeling and the hope that my involvement with Sisters is just beginning.

....

Mary Fishman is producer of the 2012 film Band of Sisters, *her first. She grew up in Chicago, spent her young adulthood as a student at the University of Notre Dame in Indiana, then worked as an architect in Chicago, in southern California, and in France. Returning home, she specialized in historic preservation and zoning for the City of Chicago's Department of Planning and Development. She left her job to help care for her mother, and began work on* Band of Sisters *in 2004.*

Compassionate Sign of the Possible

DANIEL P. HORAN, OFM

I wouldn't be who I am today if it weren't for women religious in the United States. Then again, almost none of us would be where we are or who we've become without them. If you were born in a Catholic hospital, were educated in a Catholic elementary or high school, learned about your faith from a parish religious education program, or benefited from one of the many ministries founded and maintained for centuries by women religious—oftentimes without our appropriately acknowledging them—then you are like me, a person deeply affected for the better by American Sisters.

Although they have not sought the spotlight, nor has their good work in the name of Christ and for all of us warranted the sort of negative appraisal it has recently received, I am grateful to be offered the opportunity to reflect on the ways women religious in the United States have had an impact on my life.

"A central purpose of any vocation to religious life today is to be a sign that reminds and shows the world that something is possible," a Sister of St. Joseph once said to me during a workshop. I took her point to include the possibility that such a life, challenging at times as it is, can be lived; that to honestly strive to follow Jesus's example in the Gospel is not as far-fetched as some who want to compromise it suggest, that limited human beings can still be a positive force for good in the world, and that faith is not an antiquated form of superstition, but a life-giving force in our hearts and wider communities.

Like so many others, the first memory I have of women religious goes back to my early days in elementary school. Having attended kindergarten in Connecticut the year before my family moved back to Central New York, first grade became a real adjustment because it was a new grade level in a new school in a new city.

What was also new was the presence of the women religious who staffed the parish school of Our Lady of Lourdes in Utica, New York. The Daughters of Charity, whose modified religious habit in my elementary school days no longer resembled the original "flying nun" style of ages past, worked at the school alongside an otherwise lay faculty and staff. The principal, Sister Kathleen, is the first Sister whom I remember meeting.

The scene begins with me sitting on the wooden bench in the hallway outside the principal's office. I still recall the feeling of the heavy wood beneath me as I sat in my little Catholic school uniform on the bench's edge, swinging my legs under me because they could not reach the ground. I was there against my will, but then again, few five-year-old first-graders would willingly sit outside the principal's office on their own. I had gotten in trouble during class.

My mother would later insist, half-jokingly and yet with a tone of seriousness, that I had "undiagnosed attention deficit disorder" or some similar variation, but this was before the common diagnosis of such things became prevalent. Whatever the cause, whether by boredom or my general precocious disposition, I had done something to warrant being expelled from my first-grade classroom and was now awaiting my encounter with the principal.

It's funny how so many personal stories and popular images of religious Sisters in a parochial school setting convey women who are stern, severe, mean, or somehow sadistic. I'm sure there were such instances of cruel Sisters, slapping hands with rulers and embarrassing little children for forgetting multiplication tables, but my earliest encounter with Sister

Kathleen was entirely unlike these more culturally ingrained caricatures.

Sister Kathleen was gentle and firm in her communication to me that whatever I did was unacceptable, but she did not instill the "fear of God" into me so much as she kindly challenged me to be a better little boy. It wouldn't be the last time I would get in trouble as an elementary school student, nor would it be the last time Sister Kathleen would have to speak with me about acting up in class or on the playground, but it was the last time I would be uncertain about whose side the Sisters were on. They weren't out to get me, but were deeply concerned and invested in my wellbeing and growth as a student and as a person. Even as a child I could sense this.

There was something about Sister Kathleen and the rest of the Daughters of Charity at my school that has left an indelible imprint in my memory and heart that categorized these women religious in a very positive space. Their gentleness—always grounded in their firm sense of purpose and determination—set a warm tone early on in the way I perceived religious Sisters. Beginning with Sister Kathleen and continuing for decades to come, I would associate the compassionate face of Christ with the ministry of women religious.

There is a care ministry at my family's parish (the same Our Lady of Lourdes associated with my elementary school) that consists of several volunteers who help families with planning funerals and practical concerns of end-of-life support for family members. For years, two Sisters of St. Joseph have directed this team. What is particularly notable about these two Sisters is that, in addition to both being members of the same congregation, they also happen to be biological sisters. But the similarities don't stop there; Sister Lois and Sister Elizabeth also are identical twins!

When one wonders what the compassionate face of Christ might look like, I suggest they need to look no further than Sister Lois and Sister Elizabeth. Their compassion, genuine love of their vocation, concern for all people, and desire to comfort the afflicted and console the grieving reflects the ministry of Jesus Christ in the most direct and powerful way. They used to minister in this capacity together, joined at times by retired women and men volunteers, and their presence intuitively brought a peace and comfort in their midst.

Two years ago Sister Elizabeth died. The loss of her sister, friend, and ministerial companion could not have been easy for Sister Lois, but her work with the challenging and important ministry to the ill, the dying, and the grieving needed to be carried on. There is no doubt in my mind that it was and remains her faith that enables her to continue the work of God in so many ways.

Recently, my grandfather and grandmother died within a month of each other. Their deaths were what people sometimes call a blessing, for each, in different ways, had been suffering from illness.

When my grandparents were near the end of their earthly pilgrimage, it was Sister Lois who walked with my family as we planned the funeral liturgy. In meetings with family members and during informal conversations, Sister Lois made present the Spirit of God always already in our midst. Her trust and faith in a loving and generously compassionate God served as a powerful force for good, enabling her to embrace us in our time of loss and lift us up when we were emotionally fallen.

Memories of Sister Kathleen, Sister Lois, and Sister Elizabeth for me capture in some partial way the possibility of God's generous love in difficult times.

Role Models for Christian Living

Among the myriad ways that women religious remind and show the world that something greater is possible is by their individual and collective modeling of Christian living for the rest of the Church. Time and again I have been amazed to learn the stories of women religious in the United States and abroad facing some of the most dangerous or hostile situations, selflessly entering unfamiliar and uncomfortable environments, and exercising a manner of living in the most trying circumstances in a way that can only be described as heroic.

There are the famous examples that are known worldwide (one thinks of Mother Teresa, Sister Dorothy Stang, and others), yet we also have the perhaps less dramatic but still heroic examples of Christian living in each of our lives.

I often think about the Poor Clare Sisters I've met over the years, the cloistered branch of Franciscan nuns that were founded by St. Clare of Assisi after the inspiration of St. Francis, whom I consider some of the holiest people on the planet. Committed to living a contemplative, prayerful, and quiet life, these women enter a monastery and basically remain within those limited confines for their whole life. In a society and age that values autonomy and self-sufficiency, it's awe-inspiring to come to know these women who subscribe to none of those cultural expectations, but instead embrace a life dedicated to simplicity and prayer.

What has always struck me about the Poor Clares is their collective joy. It's not some artificial veneer of happiness, but, rather, a deeply rooted sense of satisfaction and peace. My spiritual director (someone with whom I meet regularly to discuss my prayer life and spiritual journey) during novitiate was Sister Pat, a Poor Clare from New Jersey. In speaking with her about my own faith and prayer life, I was affirmed and challenged by her words and example. And I know that I am only one of many, many people who have had similar encounters with these women.

In looking for inspiration I also think about the so-called active communities of Sisters, those who work in ministries of all sorts in the community. I think of people like Sister Margaret Carney, a Franciscan Sister and president of St. Bonaventure University. She balances the complex demands that a university administrator daily encounters, while continually returning to her Franciscan spiritual roots to ground herself and those with whom she works.

I think of people like Sister Ilia Delio, a world-renowned scholar, writer, and Franciscan Sister who was one of my graduate-school mentors. As I worked on my master's thesis, she offered guidance, support, and questions that reflect an educator deeply committed to sound scholarly research. As a friend and mentor, she continues to offer me a model of how to integrate two aspects of my life: the important need to engage in sound academic work and the Franciscan challenge to reach out to a broader audience in an accessible way so that all women and men might benefit from the riches of the Christian theological tradition.

I think, too, of Sister Kate, a ninety-five-year-old Franciscan Sister with whom I have had the privilege to minister at a parish in New Jersey on visits to the infirm, shut-ins, and immobile elderly. Despite working far beyond retirement age—as so many Sisters do—Sister Kate continues to give of herself and use her energy daily for others. Her compassion and patience, her tireless commitment to those on the margins of society, and her dedication to a life of prayer and ministry challenges and inspires me to be a better Franciscan friar and a better Christian all around.

Most of all, these days I think of all the women religious in the United States who touch countless lives, alleviate the suffering of so many, strive to offer a voice to the voiceless, remember the forgotten, care for those most in need, and focus their lives on the greater good of all God's people, without concern or regard for what they could receive in return.

They are committed to living the Gospel life in the manner of what Jesus instructs in Matthew 25—clothing the naked, visiting the imprisoned, feeding the hungry. All of us, but especially the most vulnerable in our communities, would be worse off if these dedicated women had not so generously given their lives in response to God's call to a religious vocation.

....

Daniel P. Horan, OFM, is a Franciscan friar of Holy Name Province, who is currently completing a Ph.D. in systematic theology at Boston College, and serves on the board of directors of the International Thomas Merton Society. He is the author of Dating God: Live and Love in the Way of St. Francis, *and blogs regularly at DatingGod.org.*

Mi Hermana Tess

María de Lourdes Ruiz Scaperlanda

When I was an eighteen-year-old sophomore at the University of Texas in Austin, I was active in a variety of ministries at the Paulist-led Catholic Student Center. One was a student-led effort to evangelize the 48,000-student campus based on our study of the pope's 1975 encyclical on evangelization, *Evangelii Nuntiandi.*

One day in the spring, my good friend and staff member Sister Anne, a Dominican from Houston, received a call from a Franciscan Sister working in McAllen, Texas. She explained that a group from the United Farm Workers movement had come to Austin to speak to the convening Texas legislature and to lobby on behalf of farm workers. They were looking for a place to stay for a few days and wanted to connect with college students at the Catholic Student Center who were interested in learning about their ministry.

As a child, I had plenty of experience putting faith into action. My family was exiled from Cuba to Puerto Rico, where I spent most of my childhood. Many of my early memories involve visiting the convents and monasteries all over the island where my mother's friends had been relocated. These *hermanitas*—little sisters—had not only taught alongside my mom, they had known María de Jesús her entire life, and they loved to entertain me with funny and unknown stories about my mom while I feasted on their candy.

Largely through the encouragement of these relocated women religious and other Cuban priest-friends, I watched my parents' life evolve from living as newly arrived refugees to immigrants making a new life and home in Puerto Rico. My parents brought with them the energy of their experience as leaders of Pinar del Río's *Juventud de Acción Católica,* Catholic Youth in Action, joining Puerto Rico's Cursillo movement, and organizing activities and ministries through the schools and parishes.

My parents took my brother, Ignacio, and me everywhere they went. We visited prisons. We collected and repaired toys for needy children. We attended fundraising concerts for underprivileged schools. We traveled hours along the island's windy roads to events hosted by their friends to support their ministry. We hosted organizing meetings in our undersized living room, usually accompanied by my grandmother Josefita's cooking—just as it would have been done in Cuba.

So as a young adult in Texas, I was more than willing to meet these people who advocated for the farm workers.

Sister Marie-Therese Browne, or Tess, as she introduced herself, was a thirty-seven-year-old dynamo with a heart the size of Texas. She was a member of a Wisconsin-based congregation of Franciscan Sisters. A native of Trinidad, Tess and I immediately bonded as we joked and shared our experience of living in the U.S. as Hispanic women from the Caribbean islands. But as Tess pointed out in her characteristic direct style, in an accent laced by the Creole and French spoken on her island, that, as a black woman and Hispanic, "I have one up on you!"

Moving to the states as a teenager had been a challenge for me on many levels. In the Caribbean, where race was not as important as ethnicity, I was friends with whites, blacks, mestizos, and mulattos. Between 1960, the year I was born, and the 2000 census, questionnaires in Puerto Rico did not even ask about race or color. This was not so in the States, where I was shunned by blacks for being white, by Mexicans for being a *güera* (light-skinned), and by whites for my heavy accent.

In Tess, I found a sister in spirit and a Sister in Spirit.

One of the first discussions organized by Tess and the group from the

United Farm Workers union at the Catholic Student Center involved a presentation on their focused efforts lobbying against the back-breaking short-handled hoe in Texas. *El cortito,* "the short one," was an undersized hoe that forced farm workers to bend and stoop all day long in the fields—a position that led to debilitating back injuries. Although it had been banned in California in 1975, growers still argued that use of the short hoe was essential to the success of their crops.

"Growers look at human beings as implements. But if they had any consideration for the torture that people go through, they would give up the short-handled hoe," explained Sister Tess, quoting labor leader and farm worker César Chavez.

Listening to Tess's stories, I was a bit starstruck. Like that of Tom Hanks's character in *Forrest Gump,* Tess's life had casually crossed paths with significant moments in history. Picketing alongside César Chavez. Civil rights marches. A sit-in with Dorothy Day.

Over time I learned that Tess and I also shared a deep love for Mother Mary. Tess recalled, "After growing up with Mary (after whom I am named, along with St. Thérèse), praying the family rosary, and continuing that my first year in college, I turned her off in my later college years as someone who could not understand my life as a woman—a modern young woman at that. Mary and what she stood for were unattainable and somehow good, but irrelevant."

This whole image was challenged and changed on a hot day in 1975, when some other Sisters and I left the NAWR Assembly/Convention (National Assembly of Women Religious—later the Assembly of Religious Women) in San Francisco to join César and his walk for farm worker justice. César and a small group were walking over a thousand miles along highways and in and out of California farming communities.

Tess noted that Chavez wanted to highlight that the new act signed into law by Governor Jerry Brown gave farm workers in California similar dignity, recognition, and rights as other workers in the United States. Each night there would be a rally in a small farming community.

César and the Teatro Campesino and others would, by their very presence, as well as by their words, tell farm workers not to be afraid, to stand up, that they had worth and rights. Leading this whole march, each day was the banner of Our Lady of Guadalupe, carried high in front of everyone.

One day, Tess recalled, she was given the Our Lady of Guadalupe banner to carry: It was then that everything changed. "That day I entered into a new relationship with Maria—as sister, mother of us all, compañera, and much more. Mary, the unwed teenage mother. Mary, Joseph, and the child, refugees fleeing for their lives. The women and men fleeing the wars in El Salvador and Guatemala taught me much about this Mary, the refugee. Plus, she was literally their protection."

Tess frequently shocked me, provoked me, and in a very real way, inspired me. As a Hispanic privileged enough to be attending college, I felt a special responsibility to learn more, to do more for these people— my people. So when she invited students interested in visiting the Rio Grande Valley to come learn more about the work of the United Farm Workers and the life of farm workers in south Texas, I jumped at the opportunity.

Our group's visit to the border towns of San Juan and McAllen is a blur in my memory. I remember going to UFW rallies, and being the one to introduce our students in Spanish to the farm workers gathered that night. I remember celebrating daily Mass and prayers with our hosts, Tess's co-ed religious community. But what stands out the most in my memory are the intense feelings I had throughout that weekend.

It was my first time encountering a situation so tragic, so horrible, so challenging, that I felt completely powerless and ultimately, deeply angry. I was livid about living conditions of children and their families in the *colonias*—dirt streets, no running water, houses that were, truthfully, shacks. It was like being in a Third World country. I was broken-hearted and infuriated conversing in Spanish with young women my age who had already lived profoundly painful lives. And in all honesty, I was irritated with my own ignorance, for not knowing this existed just five hours from my home.

Sitting by myself in the community's chapel one night, I cried weakly in my seething anger. Sister Tess walked in and just sat next to me, waiting until I could speak. When she sensed that I was ready, she grabbed my hand and looked at me.

"How do you do it?" The words stumbled clumsily. "How can you do this work and see all this, every day, and not be consumed by the anger?"

Without hesitation, Tess began, "I don't do it. I offer up my day every morning to the One who can make a difference, and I leave the details up to God," she paused but continued to look intensely at me. "I come to the Eucharist daily and let it heal me. And every night, I leave my anger, frustration, hopelessness, despair, right here, at the foot of the altar. I am not the maker, María, I am the instrument."

Tess and her best friend and UFW coworker, Sister Carol Ann Messina, continued to work in south Texas and to make visits to Austin, giving presentations on the progress of their work to the Catholic Student Center students. The Texas legislature finally passed a measure banning the short-handled hoe in Texas in 1981, the year I graduated from college and married a fellow Longhorn, Michael. For our wedding, Sister Tess and Sister Carol gave us a biography of César Chavez—signed and addressed to both of us by Chavez himself.

The next few years, Tess and I stayed in touch through letters and late-night conversations where she would catch me up on the progress of the UFW, how they had helped pass legislation giving coverage to farm workers under workers' compensation. And I would tell her stories about my evolving family.

As my first and second child were born, Tess and Carol Ann celebrated our growing family with us. When the farm workers began a national boycott demanding better fundamental rights from grape growers, they brought Michael and me a bumper sticker that we promptly placed on our Mazda. In large bold letters, it proclaimed, "No Grapes." It was no small task explaining to a three-year-old and a one-year-old why we couldn't buy grapes at the grocery store, but Tess and Carol Ann helped me with that, too.

In 1985, on a visit to her mother in New Jersey, Carol Ann became suddenly and critically ill. She died January 14, 1985. On one side of her funeral holy card was a quote from Dag Hammarskjöld: "For all that has been: Thanks. To all that shall be: Yes." On the other side, the card read, "This is what God asks of you: to act justly; to love tenderly; to walk humbly with your God" (Micah 6:8). At their next convening, the Texas legislature unanimously passed a resolution praising Sister Carol Ann Messina, her love of the poor, and her accomplishments on behalf of farm workers in Texas.

I was not surprised to hear from Tess that she eventually decided to join Carol Ann's community, the Sisters of Charity of Nazareth, Kentucky. I knew that losing Carol Ann was very difficult for Tess, whose entire family lived in Trinidad. The Sisters of Charity and the spirit of Carol Ann that lived there became her home away from home.

Over the years, Tess and I would lose touch—then suddenly and effortlessly connect again. Our late night conversations got longer as the distance between us grew. Our family moved to Washington, D.C., and eventually back to Austin (where we had moved from Puerto Rico), while Tess traveled and ministered all over the country, making trips to Trinidad as often as she could to visit her aging mother.

God also provided us with unexpected encounters. In the summer of 1992, while serving as state correspondent for the Texas Catholic Press, I was sent to New Orleans to cover the National Black Catholic Congress. And as I checked in, there was Tess sitting in the lobby smiling at me!

After her extraordinary life, it may seem inconceivable that Sister Tess could still surprise and provoke me. Yet her ministry over the past ten years may be the most inspiring of all.

With love, patience, gratitude, and humility, I've seen Tess embrace the ministry of taking care of her aging mother, Dorothea I. Browne, another formidable island woman by any account. First Tess invited Dorothea to move near her in Boston, moving in and out of her mother's personal apartment as Dorothea needed help, yet always honoring her mother's independence and wishes.

This year when we visited in person, Tess the storyteller wowed me once again—this time, with beautiful, powerful stories about her mom's final year, how gracefully she faced pancreatic cancer, and how fearlessly she accepted death.

As we have over the last three decades, Tess and I exchanged personal stories and gifts. I gave her holy cards of Our Lady of Lourdes from my daughter Michelle's summer wedding, and she brought me holy cards and programs from her mom's funeral Mass in December. We laughed and cried over Dorothea's words of wisdom: "Some people give you a glass of water and expect you to give them champagne." "God is my source." "Do not be afraid." "Do not gossip—if you can't say something good about somebody, shut your mouth." And we giggled over her last words to Tess, "Straighten your back."

As I listened to Tess honoring her mom's memory by sharing with me her stories, I could not help but be awed once again over Tess's dedication, her embodiment of the Gospel values in the most quotidian of all ministries—caring for the aged. Living out her ministry has never been about doing charity work, or about doing glamorous work—but about being Jesus in the skin to the people in front of her, whomever that may be.

As one of my dear friends likes to say, I have lived a privileged life. In my fifty-two years, I have known, experienced, been loved by, challenged by, laughed with and lived with, some of the most remarkable religious women in the world. There are truly too many to honor in this short essay. May these words be, above all, a prayer of thanksgiving for each of them. *¡Gracias, mis queridas Hermanitas!*

···

María de Lourdes Ruiz Scaperlanda is an award-winning journalist and author from Norman, Oklahoma. Her books include The Journey: A Guide for the Modern Pilgrim.

Faithful Sisters

"Land of 10,000 Nuns"—that's what I thought when I saw the green Minnesota license plate in the church parking lot. We were in eastern Kentucky, youthful volunteers in a truly isolated small town, in those days before the highway came through that area. I couldn't help but notice how odd it was to have these cars with "Land of 10,000 Lakes" plates proclaiming a foreign presence.

This community in Lewis County seemed to be crawling with them, though really there was only a community of four or five Franciscan Sisters from Rochester, Minnesota. But these women were everywhere, it seemed, helping the very poor who showed up at the church doors daily, or heading out into the county to serve neighbors in need.

These were some of the very poor areas of Appalachia, where in the 1950s malnutrition had been apparent, and even now, in the 1970s, poverty was ubiquitous. The Sisters, with their volunteers in tow, staffed rummage stores, helped buy groceries, and provided medical transportation to the nearest hospitals, several hours away.

The Sisters' commitment to charity and simplicity was certainly a witness to this small town of Vanceburg. Even though they were from somewhere else, they didn't act like rich people. Their commitment to celibacy was a bit more confusing—local women get married, with few exceptions. But, as anywhere, the marriages don't always work out, and often women get the short end. Simpler women are sometimes sexually exploited. A former volunteer recalls a story of one local woman who chatted with her on the long drive to a regional hospital. "I'm going to be like those Catholic nuns!" the woman proclaimed. "They don't give none, and they don't get none!"

Early in the morning the Sisters were up before the pastor to be sure the tiny church was ready for morning Mass. These particular Sisters had no organist among them to play the living-room-sized organ, but the Sisters were resourceful. They put any volunteer or local parishioner who could play guitar or organ to work leading the small congregation—a few on weekdays, maybe fifty or more on a Sunday—in song.

After college my wife and I wound up in nearby Carter County, then a forty-minute back-road ride through mountain and valley from Vanceburg. There was a related mission parish there, a satellite of sorts to the tiny parish in Lewis County. The pastor, Father Pat, would commute to Carter County for Mass on the weekends. Sister Marcan, a Rochester Franciscan, was pastoral administrator for that parish in Carter County, Sts. John and Elizabeth. (Its name recalls the first two native-born American saints; one of them, St. Elizabeth Ann Seton, was foundress of the Sisters of Charity.)

The old-timers in that parish told me stories of how, years earlier, they had traveled an hour to go to Mass, even worshiped in a trailer for some years. But now they had a parish and looked to Sister Marcan to help hold things together. Marcan lived in a house near the church—I will never forget her telling tales of how bullet holes got into her house's walls at some point before she lived there. She and these other missionary Sisters were both humble and fearless.

Sister Marcan is a deeply gifted woman, but she never blew her own horn. The pastor, Fr. Pat, himself was a man of many gifts, including design, art, photography, music, and writing. He was editor of a missionary fundraising magazine, the *Glenmary Challenge*. Sometimes as he barreled across the mountain roads on the way from one project to another, Sister Marcan would sit across from him in the front seat, taking notes, reacting, and helping Fr. Pat to write his stories, under various pseudonyms, which would be read across the United States. Her name never appeared in print, and she never complained.

Responding to the needs of the local Appalachian culture, Marcan organized and ran a local summer Bible school at a nearby farm. That Bible school would draw many more families than ever would step into a Catholic church. The Catholics, fewer than one percent of the local population, were still widely distrusted, as they were across Appalachia and in many parts of the South. Marcan's goal was to build that trust, in hopes that someday some of those families might join the parish.

The parishioners in the surrounding area, and plenty of others in the community, revered Sister Marcan. She was always around the church, helping people make connections with each other, helping poor visitors find the help they needed, and keeping track of young volunteers who sometimes came to work with her.

Carter Caves State Resort Park was nearby; Marcan made sure that all was ready for the outdoor Sunday Mass held there during the tourist season, and often prepared "hobo dinners" that could be heated in the campfire for the priest, herself, and a few of the parishioners who might spend Sunday afternoon at the park.

Perhaps that sense of hospitality is the fondest memory I carry from my few years working near Sister Marcan. Unlike many larger parishes in the northern United States, people who came to Sunday Mass at Sts. John and Elizabeth often stayed around for an hour or more afterwards, sharing snacks or even potluck dishes. Sister Marcan created the space for that to happen.

In her eighties now, Marcan is long "retired" to a job in her Minnesota motherhouse at Assisi Heights, where her Sisters had recruited doctors and actually started the Mayo Clinic, on their grounds, during the nineteenth century. It is Brother Francis of Assisi (St. Francis) and his cohort Sister Clare of Assisi (St. Clare) who inspire them.

One day, just a few years ago, long after her retirement, she and another octogenarian Sister quietly checked out one of the convent's shared cars and slipped out for a two-day, twenty-hour drive to Carter County. She just wanted to check in on old friends and see how things were going in the parish. This Sister cannot be stopped.

Parachuting Nuns

A few years after my Vanceburg stint, I heard about parachuting nuns. The phrase came from a Methodist minister in Tennessee who wasn't talking about airplanes, but rather about Sisters who had shown up in small Appalachian towns, seemingly out of nowhere. "We didn't know where they came from or how they had found our tiny little towns," he said, "but they had more impact on our local communities than almost anyone else. They are incredible women." That's a fact.

During the 1980s, I worked as an advocate, helping to tell the stories of people on the bottom of our economy. I ran into scores of Sisters during those years in Appalachia and the Deep South. These were the Sisters of whom my Tennessee minister-friend spoke. Communities throughout the mountains, which generally were ignored and isolated, suddenly found small groups of Catholic Sisters moving into town. Some of these areas had scarcely seen a Catholic before, let alone a Sister.

My friend recalled, "They scratched their heads and wondered, 'How did they end up here?'" Whatever the case, he said, these women were some of the most talented and dedicated people ever to come to town. And they did tremendous good, in ways that might have been unimaginable before they arrived.

Indirectly, they ended up scattered in communities among the isolated poor because of Pope John XXIII. As part of his inspiring vision, he initiated the Second Vatican Council, to renew the Church. That worldwide council, in 1965, called for all of the religious communities, women and men, to return to the vision of their founders. It challenged religious communities to study the gift, or charism, of each community's founder and see how their modern ministries reflect that gift. For countless Sisters' and men's communities, the result of this prayerful, if at times tumultuous, reflection, was a branching out into all sorts of new ministries, especially ministry among the poor.

Pope John's staff had gone a step further, too. In seeing the great need of the Church in Latin and South America, they had called, in the early 1960s, for communities to send missionaries forth to help build up the Church there. In the United States, a decade later, the bishops of Appalachia followed suit, issuing their landmark call in a 1975 pastoral letter, *This Land Is Home to Me*, again calling for religious to come and help.

Religious communities took these summons seriously and sent people forward, both in the 1960s and again in the 1970s. Some of the best and the brightest Sisters, priests, and Brothers went to some of these most isolated and poor communities. They believed deeply they were heeding the oldest calling in the Church, Jesus's command in the Gospels to go out and bring the Good News to the "ends of the earth."

That's why there were parachuting nuns, two of whom were Sister Evelyn, a Pittsburgh Benedictine, and Sister Mary (there are lots of Sister Marys!), an Adrian (Michigan) Dominican. Both of these Sisters spent decades helping people in very poor communities learn how to understand about the bigger forces of corporate and government power that were affecting their lives, and how to speak to large institutions. The word for all of this is empowerment, the "pick up your mat and walk" type that Jesus promoted. These were two of the scores of women who dedicated their lives to it.

Along the way, they learned as much from the people they served as they taught them. Sister Evelyn loves to tell the story of the young girl who set her straight not long after she had come from Pittsburgh to work in St. Charles, in the coalfields of Virginia. Sisters from several religious communities were living together, and had set up a "ministry of presence" among the coal-mining families. The Sisters would simply live there, listen to the needs of the people, and do what they could to help. Outreach to battered women became part of their ministry.

Not long after Evelyn had arrived, there was a phone call to the Sisters. A man had beaten his wife, and had, in anger and perhaps shame, left the area, at least for a few days. The woman was badly injured and needed hospital-level medical attention. Two Sisters took the woman some miles away to the nearest hospital, and newcomer Evelyn was sent "up the holler" (mountain hollow) to tend to the children.

She arrived at the simple house where the family lived, and began chatting with the several children who lived there. She could provide some comfort to these frightened young people by cooking some food, she thought. But she could find no food. When she asked the oldest girl, a young teenager, where some food might be, she instructed Sister Evelyn: "The flour is over there." OK, thought Evelyn, now what? "The lard is over here," the girl instructed. What do I do with this? thought the Pittsburgher.

Exasperated, the girl took the lead, mixing the lard, a little milk, baking soda, salt, and flour into dough, helped Sister Evelyn roll out the dough, cut biscuits, and put them into hot lard in an iron skillet on the wood stove, after adding a little kindling atop the smoldering coal that would heat the surface just so. "Lady," the girl asked, "how did you get to be so old and be so dumb?"

In a house that had nothing more than biscuits to eat, Evelyn learned that she wouldn't have all of the answers. Bible in hand, a prayer in her heart, she went on to help many a family after that.

My friend Sister Mary would spend her years working with groups of people who were assembling community and worker organizations across Appalachia and the South. She, like many Sisters, knew how to pull people together and to help them develop an organization. With her guitar and her golden voice, she helped set the tone for social change.

In the coming years, Sisters Mary and Evelyn, along with other Church workers and scores of local people, left a legacy of community organizations in several states. The world was better for their presence.

For Love of the Earth

Somewhere around the edges of my Appalachian experience, while attending college, I met Cathy's family. Cathy and I had fallen in love at the University of Dayton, and, a few years later, while working in eastern Kentucky, gotten married.

Cathy's family had been in Pittsburgh for generations, but job opportunities had brought her parents and older sisters west to Springfield, Ohio. There the Sisters of Charity of Cincinnati took care to see that the young ones at St. Teresa Parish were well-educated. Those Sisters must have made a good impression, because over the years three of Cathy's five biological sisters entered the convent at Mount St. Joseph, near Cincinnati.

For various reasons, two moved on to other lifestyles, though their years living among the Sisters colored every bit of the lives they chose: one a college professor, the other first a specialist among teachers of disabled children, then a public-defense attorney among the poor.

The Sister who remained, Sister Mary, was my in-depth introduction to the women behind the ministries. She and Sister Paula, living in a solar-powered-apartment, quietly and unquietly witness to Gospel values. Mary is a counselor who has worked with many people, quietly helping them to name their gifts and improve their lives and relationships. After decades offering counsel, she recently became part of the community's leadership team, and is a member of the LCWR that's been in the news so much.

Her housemate, Sister Paula, now plenty old for retirement but showing few signs of slowing down, is a biology-professor-turned-futurist. Sister Paula Gonzalez is well-known in many parts of the United States for her impassioned pleas to live as responsible citizens of our planet. It was from Sister Paula that many people learned how important it is to conserve the planet's resources through appropriate technology (solar power, underground heating systems, smart construction—you name it!) in order to reuse the things of this earth. And she did this long before going green became popular.

Where the Sisters of my childhood might have reminded us to save for the starving children in China (nothing wrong with that), Paula's network of Sisters and lay workers remind us also to save the earth. Her passion is stewardship of the earth's resources, over which, she reminds us, humans were given dominion as far back as the book of Genesis.

So in the early 1980s, I put in time getting to know Cathy's "older sisters," Sister Mary and Sister Paula. At the time, that meant getting a shovel and helping Paula and her team of volunteer recruits dig the earth below an abandoned chicken coop at the motherhouse farm to install a passive heating system that would store energy collected from the sun. It was all part of "La Casa del Sol," in which Paula and Mary would demonstrate for decades that we truly can live closer to the earth and live well.

It was at Paula's place, for years, that scores of volunteers would donate and organize materials for "the world's largest yard sale" (she's an idealist). One year I spotted large stacks of hardwood flooring. This biologist had practically stood in front of bulldozers at work tearing down an old gymnasium at the nearby college, and pleaded with the operators to save the wood—it could be reused! And it was. Here was Paula, another unstoppable force for right.

Trust in Providence

Hardworking, humble, determined, resourceful—let me tell you about one more group of Sisters I know. Up the Ohio River a few miles from La Casa del Sol, past Cincinnati, on the Kentucky side, is a motherhouse of the Congregation of Divine Providence. Anyone who has seen the film *Rain Man* will recognize the grounds—the motherhouse temporarily became a mental-health institution, the site where Tom Cruise's character went to visit his autistic brother, played by Dustin Hoffman. Some will remember the tree-lined road where the brothers walked and talked. In real life, it's the motherhouse drive.

Sister Mary Luke, Sister Mary Immaculate, Sister Mary Thomas, Sister Alice and others—these women taught and worked in nearby St. Bernard Parish and St. Bernard School, where our older sons, now college graduates, began their formal education.

I've never seen so much good done with so few financial resources. These women were determined to serve this urban neighborhood and this tiny school that had seen better days. "Trust in providence," were the words I heard over and over again from these Sisters.

Sister Mary Immaculate—"Mac" to her close friends—taught the first-graders to make a prayer corner in their homes where they could focus their youthful energies. At least they did so in the prayer corner in her classroom. "You are children of God," she would exclaim to rambunctious little ones, "now act like it!"

Sister Mary Thomas, from Ireland, devoted herself each year to the crowd-pleasing and child-educating Christmas reenactment of the nativity story. And Sister Mary Luke, school principal, quietly devoted her days to keeping the whole boat afloat. She was house superior and provided music for the parish when she wasn't being principal.

These women lived in former classrooms above the school, converted into a makeshift convent. From them I learned how their Sisters had started their branch of the Sisters of Divine Providence in Kentucky, inspired by the life of a French priest, John Martin Moye, who worked with the poor. As did women in religious communities across the United States, the Sisters farmed the land surrounding the motherhouse and depended upon nearby Catholics to help financially.

Sister Alice has devoted her later career to helping others cry out for justice. In our area we see her in the news once in a while, whether she's supporting an inner-city housing initiative, or leading a protest outside the death-house door at the state penitentiary. This "radical nun," though, is the same woman I saw in St. Bernard Church one day, artist's paintbrush in hand, touching up chipped spots on the statue of the Blessed Mother. Go figure.

To say they live a simple life at the motherhouse is an understatement. Every dime is accounted for. The food is homemade. The women share automobiles. Younger Sisters (now mostly older than midlife) care for the older ones (women who might well have finally retired in their late seventies).

Consider, during the filming of *Rain Man* at the Divine Providence motherhouse, when the crew realized they needed a coffee can for an upcoming scene. Someone drove into town and bought a can of coffee, brought it back, and opened it. Just as he was preparing to dump the coffee into the trash—they needed an empty can—a Sister, looking on, screamed, "Stop!" She raced to the kitchen, grabbed a Ziploc bag, and saved the coffee.

Most Sisters live like that, whether in small communities or large. They pray a lot. They work at working together. They try their hardest to live simply—sometimes without much choice, due to real poverty. Those who have more resources help those who haven't. All of them embrace simplicity as a radical commitment to Gospel values, and offer that faithful witness to the rest of us.

John Feister is editor-in-chief of St. Anthony Messenger *magazine and other periodicals at Franciscan Media, for whom he's interviewed people across this country and internationally over the past twenty-five years. He adapted several of Richard Rohr's talks into books, including* Things Hidden: Scripture as Spirituality. *More recently he coauthored, with Franciscan Sister Charlene Smith,* Thea's Song: The Life of Thea Bowman.

Sister Janet

MAUREEN ORTH

With her white spiky hair, her black boots, and the energy of someone half her age, Sister Janet Harris was not the seventy-seven-year-old nun I had pictured who taught high school in Los Angeles some thirty years ago in California with my late aunt, also a Presentation Sister. Guilt had driven me to meet her for coffee on a September Saturday morning in Washington, D.C.

A day earlier an envelope had sailed through my mail slot inviting me to the screening of *Mario's Story*, a feature-length documentary about a young man in Los Angeles who was tried as an adult at age seventeen and sentenced to two consecutive life sentences for murder. Because of the dramatic campaign Sister Janet set in motion to free this young Latino from what she saw as an unjust and wrongful conviction—a struggle that has taken almost a decade and is not over yet—Mario Rocha's sentence was vacated by the California Court of Appeals, an extraordinary outcome that happens less than one percent of the time. Now twenty-eight, he's out on one million dollars' bail.

Sister Janet first got in touch with me after my aunt, Sister Agnes, passed away a few years ago. She and my aunt had taught together in the 1970s at a girls' high school in downtown Los Angeles, where my reticent aunt had persevered in teaching Latin and biology in the face of gangs and graffiti. Over our coffee together, with the charm she brings to her work on behalf of juvenile offenders, Sister Janet drew me into her world as if we were old friends.

She grew up in Upper Manhattan in an Irish, Italian, and Jewish neighborhood; she wanted to become a Broadway actress, but her awakening to the Church had already begun at the nearby Cloisters museum of medieval art—the illuminated manuscripts of the monks enthralled her. Art led her to God. A few years after her father, a merchant seaman, moved the family west to San Francisco, Janet, seventeen, entered the teaching order of the Presentation Sisters.

In the early 1970s, teaching in downtown Los Angeles, she allowed neighborhood gangs to use the school's playing fields every Saturday. At the time, she was pursuing a master's degree in communications at Loyola University; for her thesis she decided to make a film about the 18th Street gang and the Temple Street gang. Watching them from the bleachers week after week, she became adept at knowing when kids were lying and when they were telling the truth. And she won their trust.

"But I was naive," she told me. "I understood teenagers, but I didn't understand what was happening on the street." On one occasion, shots rang out from a car—and one of the boys pushed her out of the way. "He put himself in front of me," she told me. He was the one they were after. A week later the boy was killed. Another time, she said, "the police were putting terrible pressure on me to tell them what I knew about a gang crime." She refused and was arrested, thereby demonstrating her loyalty to the gang members and shaming the kids into telling what they knew so she could be released: "I knew my willingness to go to jail would be the catalyst to get the kids to talk," she said. "I got a lot of mileage out of that, believe me. It was not an impulsive decision."

In the late 1970s, the Los Angeles County probation department offered Sister Janet a job as a counselor to gangs—someone who would listen to their stories and act as a sounding board. As she talked to me, I was struck by the familial way she dealt with the Almighty. Sometimes, she said, when something untenable has gone on too long, "you just have to tell him off! Tell him you've had enough. I tell him off all the time."

She deplores how fecklessly boys like Mario—who she says was misidentified as a gang member—get tried as adults and sent away forever. She keeps up a running dialogue with her favorite saints about the kids she defends. Recently, coming across a group of plaster St. Francis statues at a garden nursery, she told him firmly, "'Francis, you wouldn't be a statue hanging around gardens if you were judged today on what you did in your youth.' Francis was an incorrigible youth," Sister Janet reminded me. "He was a sinner; they would have put him away for life."

That night I met Sister Janet at the screening of *Mario's Story*, which by then had won the Audience Award for Best Documentary Feature at the L.A. Film Festival. The movie makes patent the failures of the California juvenile justice system, which allows inexperienced prosecutors to decide whether boys and girls as young as fourteen are to be tried as juveniles or as adults, who can then be locked away for life.

Mario's conviction, we discover, was based on the testimony of one "eyewitness," who accused him of wielding a gun at a keg party where a seventeen-year-old youth from their gang-riddled neighborhood in East Los Angeles was killed. In a series of jailhouse interviews, Mario, tall, soft-spoken, and articulate, seems neither angry nor bitter, though he has clearly absorbed what the stakes are when you're tried as an adult: "They give you a double life sentence, and in the state of California I would never be paroled unless there is a dramatic revolution in the system. So, realistically, a double life sentence becomes a death sentence."

Sister Janet first met Mario Rocha in 1996, when she was serving as chaplain for the Los Angeles Central Juvenile Hall, the locked facility where hundreds of teenagers charged and convicted of crimes await trial and sentencing. Mario spent more than two years there. Sister Janet was supervising the hall's religious services and volunteers; she noticed

Mario right away and arranged for him to participate in the writing program called InsideOut she had helped found. His teacher was a *Los Angeles Times* reporter, Duane Noriyuki, whom Sister Janet recruited for the program. Although Mario had been well on his way to dropping out of high school, in juvenile hall he was a star pupil.

Sister Janet began to save Mario's writings ("I look out my tainted window, absorbing the dark abandoned field, and I ask myself what kind of life is this? I stare at the large trees that distantly surround these buildings and think this is not the way I want to live"). She undertook her own investigation of the murder he was accused of and became so convinced of his innocence that she was able to persuade the lawyers in the white-shoe Los Angeles law firm of Latham & Watkins to take his case *pro bono*; they also gave Mario a lie-detector test, which he passed.

Around that time, documentary filmmaker Susan Koch happened to hear Sister Janet discussing the case; then and there Koch decided to do a film on Mario, never dreaming that the firm's effort to overturn Mario's conviction would involve eight years of frustrating twists and turns—arguing motions, waiting for decisions, trying new tactics. The film, codirected by Jeff Werner, shows the extreme difficulty of freeing anyone once convicted, even with extraordinary resources at your disposal—Latham & Watkins has spent more than a million dollars on the case.

In the end, the California Appeals Court ruled that the lawyer Mario's family hired after mortgaging their home was so ineffective as to undermine the integrity of his trial. He failed to find witnesses to refute the single eyewitness, who, as Sister Janet's investigation revealed, had little credibility. The lawyer also failed to point out that although the eyewitness testified that the shooter fired the gun with his left hand, Mario is right-handed. And the lawyer did not ask that Mario, who did not belong to a gang, be tried separately from the two gang members who were also tried for the murder.

The film ends in August 2006 as Mario is released from prison, but the L.A. district attorney's office has vowed to put Mario on trial again—as early as this spring. "It's really pushing the ethical boundaries," Sister Janet charges. "They are going to try to smear him as a Latino gang member and hope a jury will seize on that."

Onscreen, Sister Janet combines serenity and steeliness. Her calm belies her anguish at seeing more and more girls and boys in their early to mid-teens subjected to harsh adult sentences, particularly in California, where a powerful union of corrections officers supported by rich building interests lobbies to keep prisons full and new ones under construction. Young people sent to adult facilities, Sister Janet argues, "often don't have the emotional and moral strength to survive. Some do, but drugs are so available. I've seen young people just give up and start using drugs."

Many young offenders, she points out, have been manipulated by the sociopaths they find themselves among. She feels that adolescents should be held to a different standard than adults, citing studies showing that adolescents' brains are not fully developed; human brains develop into the early twenties. These young people deserve a system of their own, she believes. Justice for juveniles is at stake.

It was evident from the thoughtful questions at the end of *Mario's Story* that the audience was deeply moved. Afterward I told Sister Janet I was naturally curious to meet Mario, who has recently been awarded the prestigious PEN USA fellowship, Emerging Voices, while his legal fate is being determined. When Sister Janet and I discovered quite felicitously that we would both be in California at the same time, her blue eyes sparkled. "I think God is showing off a bit." She arranged to have me invited to a lunch at the beach house of the chair of the writing program's advisory board in Malibu. There I would meet not only Mario but another graduate of the InsideOut program.

The first guest to show up on the appointed day was Walter McMillan, an engaging twenty-seven-year-old African American medical student who is president of the InsideOut writers alumni association. He and Mario were in class together in 1997, but McMillan was tried as a juvenile for robbery and served four years in a juvenile jail. He credits Sister Janet and the writing program for getting him physically and psychologically out of the South Central Los Angeles neighborhood where, according to Walter, his mother was on crack and he himself was shot at twice walking down the street.

After getting his undergraduate degree in English at the University of Washington, McMillan is now studying nuclear medicine. "In juvenile hall," he told me, "the system says you are bad, bad, bad. How empowering to discover, 'No, I'm not!' The writing helped me connect to that question, 'Who am I?'" Sister Janet went on to say: "Reading their stories in front of their peers and having their writing affirmed means more to these boys and girls than we can imagine. And the more their stories are appreciated, the more they allow themselves to be vulnerable in their writing. The kids are very good at picking up on b.s. They know that whatever they say has to come from the truth—because the others will call them on it."

Another guest at lunch was Javier Stauring, the forty-five-year-old former gemologist who succeeded Sister Janet as chaplain at juvenile hall and whom she first recruited there as a volunteer. Stauring, who acts as a mentor to Mario, had brought him to the beach lunch. Mario was grinning from ear to ear—as if he still could not quite believe he was free. (He had spent his first night out of jail in ten and a half years sleeping on his family's garage roof, looking at the stars.) There beside the ocean, he and Sister Janet hugged and laughed—in prison they had often fantasized that someday Mario would be free and they would walk on the beach together. That day had arrived.

Listening to Mario talk about books, about writing and his plans for the future, it was apparent how much Sister Janet's support and his writing teacher's encouragement had meant to him. In an essay titled "Unfit," Mario wrote: "When I joined the InsideOut writing class, I searched for words to expose the cave of my soul. I wrote about memories and painful experiences. I poured forth my fears, doubts, and perplexities on paper, and I began to understand my life, who I was and why."

For someone who had just emerged from prison and didn't know if he would be forced to go back behind bars for life, Mario seemed remarkably relaxed. "I'm confident justice will be served. I'm living proof we can correct a wrong," he told me. He calls Sister Janet "my trumpet" and claims, "She heard me for the first time." He told Susan Koch, the documentary filmmaker, that for him Sister Janet personified the Beatles song "Let It Be": There will be an answer, let it be, let it be.

"Sister Janet has a preferential love for the marginal, and one of her most powerful qualities is her yearning for justice, for the right things to happen," says Javier Stauring. He has seen firsthand how fiercely Sister Janet defends her charges. He was present one day when she pleaded with the hall's superintendent not to send a certain boy to the adult county jail. The superintendent, papers in hand, refused to change his mind. "She grabbed for the papers and tore them up: 'You're not sending him anywhere!'" For a moment, the superintendent was stunned. Then he started to laugh, Stauring recalls, "and the kid stayed there."

In 2003 Human Rights Watch determined that the plight of incarcerated youth in the Los Angeles County Men's Central Jail was among the worst in the world and honored Stauring with their Human Rights

Watch Award for his work. Speaking in Berlin before a group of international human rights activists, Stauring told them that the United States had more than 2,225 teenagers sentenced as adults to life in prison without parole. The participants removed their earpieces, thinking that they must have misheard or that the translator had made a mistake; at the time, the rest of the world had only twelve such cases. To compound the irony, according to a study Stauring sent me done by the non-profit Center on Juvenile and Criminal Justice, juvenile arrests in California's eight major cities in 2005 were at a thirty-year low.

After lunch, Stauring, Sister Janet, Ian Graham—the young lawyer formerly with Latham & Watkins who is still working on Mario's case—and Mario took a walk on the beach. The sun was shining and dolphins frolicked not far from shore. "Being near the ocean was a poetic moment, an image of freedom," Sister Janet told me later. "That's a sacred image." Back at the house, while Mario hosed the sand off his feet, I asked him how he felt. "I'm ecstatic," he said.

That night I drove past the glittering lights of downtown Los Angeles to the grim Eastlake Juvenile Hall to observe two of the approximately thirty weekly writing classes taught by the InsideOut volunteers. Each week these classes reach out to about three hundred youths in several juvenile facilities. I saw teenagers who were awaiting court dates and sentences that may lock them up for decades reading George Rodriguez and Maya Angelou—boys who were gang members, girls who cut themselves—and I alternately winced at their pain and marveled at what flowed from their pencils, at their pride in reading out loud the raw details of their sorrows, the flashes of insight, the dark realities so many of us never have to contemplate.

Sister Janet told me of her deep belief in the sacredness of every person, no matter how lost: "I approach every person looking for that."

How does she manage to do what she does? "I don't believe in hierarchies," she said, "I believe in circles. The metaphor for what I do is jazz. I find good people and let them play their instruments."

But doesn't she get discouraged? I remembered what she said the morning we met. "I'm not sure whether I believe in voices or not," she told me, "but I was driving down the freeway one day and I was having such a bad day I just cried out, 'Oh Mother of God!' Then, you know what? A very calm voice came inside me and said, 'Janet, keep your eye on the road.'"

Maureen Orth is an award-winning journalist, a special correspondent for Vanity Fair *magazine, and the founder of the Marina Orth Foundation, which promotes advanced learning in technology and English for over 1,200 students. She began her journalism career at Newsweek in 1972, where she was the pop music writer, the entertainment and lifestyle editor, and wrote seven cover stories on such music icons as Bob Dylan, Stevie Wonder, and Bruce Springsteen. In the last two decades she has traveled the world for* Vanity Fair, *reporting on a wide range of both heroes and rogues. Among the heads of state she has interviewed are Vladimir Putin and Margaret Thatcher, Argentine President Carlos Menem, Irish President Mary Robinson, and the First Lady of France, Carla Bruni. Orth's late husband of twenty-five years was NBC journalist Tim Russert; she is the mother of MSNBC's Luke Russert.*

Saintly Women

Here's a sampling of Sisters, all recognized as saints, who overcame misunderstanding and obstacles in their works of service. Thanks to Judy Ball, founding online editor of Saint of the Day, for these vignettes.

St. Mary MacKillop (1842–1909)

Mary MacKillop would be a newsmaker if she were alive today. Independent and determined, Australia's first saint aroused the ire of some rather powerful churchmen in her role as cofounder and superior of the Sisters of St. Joseph, who dedicated themselves to teaching the poor. She even was excommunicated for a time.

As her congregation grew, so did Mary MacKillop's problems. There are charges that her excommunication was related to her reporting child abuse by a local priest. Or were some members of the local hierarchy suspicious of the Sisters' work and their ownership of property? Or was it all of the above?

Questions remain about the causes of her five-month excommunication, but not about Mary's response: She held firm to her principles of right and wrong, to the Church she so loved and to the belief that her new congregation should look to Rome, rather than local bishops, to resolve key issues.

In the end, she and her Sisters offered social services that few, if any government agencies in Australia could. They served poor Protestants, Catholics, Aborigines, unmarried mothers, and orphaned children.

St. Margaret of Cortona (1247–1297)

The life of St. Margaret of Cortona would be perfect for the Lifetime channel on cable TV or as a Monday night movie: a beautiful, spirited young girl loses her mother early in life, grows into a rebellious teen, runs off with a handsome young nobleman and bears him a son. After nine years as his mistress, she discovers the body of her lover, murdered by his enemies.

End of story? Hardly. Returning home, humbled and penitent, Margaret was banished by her father and stepmother as a woman of ill repute. She then approached the Franciscan friars and, under their guidance, began a life of public penance and service. Margaret spent the rest of her years serving the sick and poor while living among them, devoting herself to prayer and calling others to the same path of conversion. She founded a community of Franciscan Sisters.

Margaret of Cortona is the patron of the homeless, of single mothers, and of midwives—and of anyone who has turned away from a sinful life.

St. Josephine Bakhita (1868–1947)

Josephine Bakhita was sold into slavery multiple times in her native Sudan, but she lived long enough to taste freedom and to serve another Master. The more than one hundred razor scars she carried on her body throughout her life never broke her spirit.

Ultimately freed from bondage when the family that owned her moved to Italy, where slavery was illegal, Josephine was drawn to the Catholic faith. At twenty-one, she was received into the Church. Several years later she entered the novitiate of the Daughters of Charity, also known as the Canossian Sisters.

For almost fifty years she served as cook, seamstress, and doorkeeper at their convents in Italy. This woman of faith and forgiveness was noted for her gentle presence and her willingness to undertake any task, however menial. Like so many women religious, she stood up for her rights, but served quietly nonetheless.

At her canonization in 2000, Pope John Paul II called her "a shining advocate of genuine emancipation."

St. Teresa of Avila (1515–1582)

She struggled with serious and mysterious health problems, with difficulties in prayer, and with the task of reforming religious life as she found it in her Carmelite monastery in Spain—lax and full of distractions. But St. Teresa of Avila placed her trust in God and persisted.

She became a woman of deep prayer and contemplation who achieved profound union with God; her writings—*Way of Perfection* and *The Interior Castle*—are classics. It was in prayer that she heard God's call to undertake reform of Carmelite life. Despite serious opposition, she was able to establish new foundations, mostly for women, that strictly adhered to her congregation's original way of life, where the emphasis was on contemplation and simple living.

Almost four hundred years after her death, St. Teresa of Avila was proclaimed a doctor of the Church, the first woman to be so recognized. She was a reformer ahead of her time.

St. Mother Theodora Guerin (1798–1856)

Lifelong frail health; the arduous life of a missionary in early America; chronic lack of funds and food; a bishop who vacillated between ignoring her and undermining her authority. Mother Theodore Guerin, as she was then known, had every reason to wonder if her trust in God's providence was misplaced. But she didn't waver. She went forward in faith.

She even returned to her native France to raise funds when her bishop refused to offer the financial support he had promised. Meanwhile, he used the occasion of her extended absence to attempt a takeover of her community. It didn't work. Mother Theodore was reelected superior, and the bishop ultimately resigned.

Against all odds, Mother Theodore lived to see a thriving religious congregation (the Sisters of Providence), schools and orphanages for needy boys and girls in parts of the Midwest, and the first Catholic women's college in the United States, St. Mary-of-the-Woods.

Faith can do that. It did for St. Mother Theodora.

St. Marianne Cope (1838–1918)

Marianne Cope considered herself a "chosen one"—chosen to serve the sick and suffering.

Those were the very words she used in accepting an invitation in 1883 to minister to people suffering from the dreaded Hansen's disease, or leprosy, in the Hawaiian Islands. Then forty-five and provincial of the Sisters of St. Francis in Syracuse, New York, she headed west with six other members of her community in 1883. They carried on the work in Hawaii of the heroic Damien of Molokai, beloved today as "St. Damien of the Lepers." He died of the contagious disease six months after the Sisters and Mother Marianne arrived.

Life changed for her—and for the women, men and children under her loving care. Drawing on her natural administrative skills, her serenity, and her compassion for all God's children, she brought hope and joy as well as new standards of cleanliness and respect into the lives of those she was chosen to serve. She could often be found comforting a patient at his or her bedside. She was fearless in the face of a disease that frightened so many. She never returned home, but, rather, died a natural death after thirty years of service to the leper colony.

Known as Mother Marianne for most of her religious life, she became a mother to countless numbers of God's special children.

St. Margaret Mary Alacoque (1647–1690)

Sister Margaret Mary Alacoque was hardly the type to call attention to herself. Humble, simple, she struggled to master the meditation style expected of her as a young Visitation Sister.

But God asked big things of her. Over a thirteen-month period at her convent in France, she told her religious superiors, Jesus repeatedly appeared to her, urging her to reveal God's love and mercy for all humankind. The visions, she explained, also called on her to persuade Church authorities to have a special feast in honor of the Sacred Heart of Jesus, along with special devotions.

The response was skepticism from members of her community. Theologians, called in to review her claims, went one better, calling the visions nothing more than simple delusions.

With the support and encouragement of her Jesuit confessor and her own unflagging faith, she pressed on. The feast of the Sacred Heart of Jesus, a worldwide devotion celebrating the mercy of God, is observed on the Friday after the feast of Corpus Christi. It's a tribute to Mary Margaret Alacoque's courage and her trust in God.

Judy Ball is a freelance writer and editor living in Cincinnati, Ohio. She served on the staff of Franciscan Media (then St. Anthony Messenger Press) from 1996 to 2009. She was educated by Sisters of Mercy, Ursulines and Jesuits.

Binka Le Breton runs the Iracambi Rainforest Research Center (Iracambi, Brazil), lectures, and broadcasts internationally on rainforest and human rights topics. She is also president of *Amigos de Iracambi*, one of a number of small nonprofits working to conserve the priceless resources of the rainforest while improving the economic situation of the local people. In her spare time she writes books, including *The Greatest Gift: the Courageous Life and Death of Sister Dorothy Stang* (Doubleday). Her other books include *Voices from the Amazon* (Kumarian), *Trapped: Modern-Day Slavery in the Brazilian Amazon* (Kumarian), and *Where the Road Ends: A Home in the Brazilian Rainforest* (Thomas Dunne).

John Feister is editor in chief of *St. Anthony Messenger* magazine and other periodicals at Franciscan Media, for whom he's interviewed people across this country and internationally over the past twenty-five years. He adapted several of Richard Rohr's talks into books: *Radical Grace, Sermon on the Mount, Hope Against Darkness,* and *Things Hidden,* all from Franciscan Media. More recently he coauthored, with Franciscan Sister Charlene Smith, *Thea's Song: The Life of Thea Bowman* (Orbis).

Mary Fishman's filmmaking debut *is Band of Sisters*. She attended Catholic elementary and high schools where sisters were her teachers, but it was during the making of this film that they became her friends—and they're still her teachers. In her previous career Mary was an architect and urban planner. She grew up in Chicago, spent her young adulthood as a student at the University of Notre Dame in Indiana; and as an architect in Chicago, in southern California, and in France. After returning home, she specialized in historic preservation and zoning for the City of Chicago's Department of Planning and Development. She left her job to help care for her mother, and began work on *Band of Sisters* in 2004. Making films is a dream come true for Mary, she says, joining her love of movies with her desire to work for social justice.

Daniel P. Horan, OFM, is a Franciscan friar of Holy Name Province, who is currently completing a PhD in Systematic Theology at Boston College, and serves on the Board of Directors of the International Thomas Merton Society. He previously taught in the department of religious studies at Siena College and has been a visiting professor in the department of theology at St. Bonaventure University. The author of more than thirty scholarly and popular articles in a variety of journals, his most recent books include *Dating God: Live and Love in the Way of St. Francis* (Franciscan Media) and *Francis of Assisi and the Future of Faith: Exploring Franciscan Spirituality and Theology in the Modern World* (Tau). He writes regularly at his blog *DatingGod.org.*

Liz Scott Monaghan recently retired after more fifteen years as an instructor of journalism and adviser to the student media at Loyola University, New Orleans. She is a columnist and contributing editor for *New Orleans Magazine,* and the author of two humor books published by St. Martin's Press, and a more recent one, *Never Clean Your House During Hurricane Season.* She has won numerous awards, both local and national, for her own writing, both humorous and serious.

Maurice J. Nutt, C.Ss.R., D.Min., earned a doctor of ministry degree in preaching from Aquinas Institute of Theology and is a noted revival, mission, and retreat preacher both nationally and internationally. Father

Nutt is also a faculty member at the Institute for Black Catholic Studies (IBCS) at Xavier University in New Orleans, Louisiana, where he teaches preaching. Currently Father Nutt is a member of the Redemptorist Parish Mission Team based in Chicago.

Maureen Orth is an award winning journalist, a Special Correspondent for *Vanity Fair Magazine*, and the founder of the Marina Orth Foundation, which promotes advanced learning in technology and English for over 1,200 students.

Orth began her journalism career as the third female writer at *Newsweek* in 1972, where she was the pop music writer, the entertainment and lifestyle editor and wrote seven cover stories on such music icons as Bob Dylan, Stevie Wonder and Bruce Springsteen. In the last two decades she has traveled the world for *Vanity Fair*, reporting on a wide range of both heroes and rogues. Among the heads of state she has interviewed are Vladimir Putin and Margaret Thatcher, Argentine President Carlos Menem, Irish President Mary Robinson, and the First Lady of France, Carla Bruni. Over a twelve-year period (1994-2006) she made headlines writing five investigative pieces on Michael Jackson. She received a 2011 Front Page Award for her article on the fight over designer Oleg Cassini's will and a national magazine award nomination for her chronicle of the zigzagging career of Arianna Huffington.

Fr. John S. Rausch, a Glenmary priest, is an award-winning writer who pursues social ministry from his home in Stanton, Kentucky. Currently he directs the Catholic Committee of Appalachia, where he has worked for over thirty-five years. In 2007 Fr. Rausch won the Teacher of Peace Award from Pax Christi, USA.

Cokie Roberts is a journalist and author. She is a contributing senior news analyst for National Public Radio as well as a regular roundtable analyst for the current *This Week With George Stephanopoulos*. Roberts also works as a political commentator for ABC News, serving as an on-air analyst for the network.

She has won countless awards in broadcast journalism over forty years, including three Emmys, and she is cited as one of the fifty greatest women in the history of broadcasting. Her mother, Lindy Boggs, was U.S. Ambassador to the Vatican from 1997–2001. Her late father was House Majority Leader Hale Boggs.

Steven V. Roberts is a journalist, writer, and political commentator. He was a senior writer at *U.S. News & World Report* for seven years where he is now a contributing editor. As a Washington pundit, Roberts appears regularly on *ABC Radio, Washington Week in Review, CNN, Hardball with Chris Matthews*. He often fills in as substitute host of *The Diane Rehm Show* on National Public Radio. He also appears regularly on *America Abroad*. Roberts has taught journalism and political communication at The George Washington University's School of Media and Public Affairs since 1997.

The Robertses write a nationally syndicated column syndicated by United Media in newspapers around the United States, and are contributing writers for *USA Weekend*, a Sunday magazine that appears in five hundred newspapers nationwide. In February 2000 they jointly published *From This Day Forward*, about their interfaith marriage and the idea of marriage through the lens of their own relationship.

María de Lourdes Ruiz Scaperlanda is an award-winning journalist and author, and contributor to numerous books. Her books include, *The Journey: A Guide for the Modern Pilgrim*. She lives in Norman, Oklahoma, with her husband of thirty years, Michael.

Adriana Trigiani is a novelist, television writer, producer, and film director. She was a writer for *The Cosby Show* and its spin-off series *A Different World* before beginning on novels. In 1996, she won the "Most Popular Documentary" award at the Hamptons International Film Festival for directing the *Queens of the Big Time*. The following year, she served as coproducer on the documentary film *Green Chimneys*.

In 2001, Trigiani wrote a novel about her hometown titled *Big Stone Gap*, based on a screenplay by the same name she authored. It was followed by three sequels, *Big Cherry Holler, Milk Glass Moon,* and *Home to Big Stone Gap*. Aside from that series, she has written *Rococo, Queen of the Big Time*, and *Lucia, Lucia*, which became a bestseller in Britain. *Very Valentine*, was published in February 2009, and followed by *Brava Valentine* in 2010. Her newest novel is *The Shoemaker's Wife* (HarperCollins).

Teresa Wilson is former leader of the Grail, a women's lay organization of about 1,000 women in twenty countries, committed to social transformation. She also was a founding organizer of Pennsylvania Peace Links. She now is retired and living in Claremont, California.